D0665843

Sharia Law or
'One Law For All'?

Sharia Law or
'One Law For All?'

Denis MacEoin
David G. Green (Editor)

Foreword by
Neil Addison

Civitas: Institute for the Study of Civil Society
London

First Published June 2009
© Neil Addison:
Sharia Tribunals in Britain—Mediators or Arbitrators?

All other material © Civitas 2009
77 Great Peter Street
London SW1P 2EZ
Civitas is a registered charity (no. 1085494)
and a company limited by guarantee, registered in
England and Wales (no. 04023541)

email: books@civitas.org.uk
All rights reserved

ISBN 978-1-906837-08-2

Independence: Civitas: Institute for the Study of Civil
Society is a registered educational charity (No.
1085494) and a company limited by guarantee (No.
04023541). Civitas is financed from a variety of private
sources to avoid over-reliance on any single or small
group of donors.

All publications are independently refereed. All the
Institute's publications seek to further its objective of
promoting the advancement of learning. The views
expressed are those of the authors, not of the Institute.

Typeset by
Civitas
Printed in Great Britain by
The Cromwell Press Group
Trowbridge, Wiltshire

Contents

Authors

Neil Addison is a practising barrister and the author of *Religious Discrimination and Hatred Law*, Taylor Francis Publishers, 2006.

He runs the website www.ReligionLaw.co.uk, and the Blog http://religionlaw.blogspot.com

David G. Green is the Director of Civitas. His books include *The New Right: The Counter Revolution in Political, Economic and Social Thought*, Wheatsheaf, 1987; *Reinventing Civil Society*, IEA, 1993; *Community Without Politics: A Market Approach to Welfare Reform*, IEA, 1996; *We're (Nearly) All Victims Now*, Civitas, 2006 and *Individualists Who Co-operate*, Civitas, 2009.

He writes occasionally for newspapers, including in recent years pieces in *The Times, The Sunday Times,* the *Sunday Telegraph* and the *Daily Telegraph*.

Dr Denis MacEoin holds degrees from Trinity College, Dublin, Edinburgh University and Cambridge (King's College). From 1979-80, he taught at Mohammed V University in Fez, Morocco, before taking up a post as lecturer in Arabic and Islamic Studies at Newcastle. In 1986, he was made Honorary Fellow in the Centre for Islamic and Middle East Studies at Durham University. He has published extensively on Islamic topics, contributing to the *Encyclopaedia of Islam*, the *Oxford Encyclopaedia of Islam in the Modern World*, the *Encyclopaedia Iranica*, the *Penguin Handbook of Living Religions*, journals, festschrifts and books, and has himself written a number of books including *The Sources for Babi History and Doctrine, Rituals in Babism and Baha'ism,* and *The Messiah of Shiraz: Studies in Early and Middle Babism*; he has also edited *Islam in the Modern World* with Ahmad al-Shahi. In 2007 he published *The Hijacking of British Islam*, a study of hate literature found in UK mosques, and his report *Music, Chess and Other Sins* was published online by Civitas in 2009. In 1992 HarperCollins published a volume of his journalism under the title *New Jerusalems: Islam, Religious Fundamentalism, and the Rushdie Affair.* He has written 25 novels and is translated into some 15 languages.

Foreword

Sharia Tribunals in Britain — Mediators or Arbitrators?

Both the Archbishop of Canterbury and the Lord Chief Justice ran into controversy in 2008 by appearing to suggest that sharia courts or tribunals should be given a role in the settlement of disputes. Part of the controversy, of course, arises from the fact that 'sharia law' in its fullness covers both criminal as well as civil law though, in fairness, both speakers were directing their remarks at the possible role of sharia tribunals as a mechanism of Alternative Dispute Resolution (ADR), especially in the settlement of matrimonial and family disputes. A similar suggestion was reportedly made, though to less publicity, by the former Chairman of the Bar Mr Stephen Hockman QC.[1]

The Archbishop in his speech said:

> there are ways of looking at marital disputes, for example, which provide an alternative to the divorce courts as we understand them. In some cultural and religious settings they would seem more appropriate.[2]

---

1 See:
http://www.telegraph.co.uk/news/newstopics/politics/lawandorder/3523672/Sharia-lawshould-be-introduced-into-legal-system-says-leading-barrister.html

2 http://www.guardian.co.uk/uk/2008/feb/07/religion.world3

Whilst the LCJ said:

> There is no reason why principles of sharia law, or any other
> religious code, should not be the basis for mediation or other
> forms of alternative dispute resolution.[3]

This was then followed by press reports that sharia 'courts' were already operating in Britain, in particular in the form of the Muslim Arbitration Tribunal (MAT).[4] The 'revelation' that these 'courts' were having their arbitration decisions (fatwas[5]) enforced by the state courts, in accordance with the Arbitration Act 1996 has led to campaigns to ban all religious tribunals from operating under the Arbitration Act.[6]

What I would suggest as also part of the reason for this public controversy is that both the Archbishop and the LCJ, together with the Muslim Arbitration Tribunal (MAT), have confused and merged together two separate and distinct ADR concepts, namely mediation and arbitration.

---

3 http://www.matribunal.com/downloads/LCJ_speech.pdf

4 www.matribunal.com

5 A 'Fatwa' is the traditional title for a Sharia legal judgement or legal opinion. Sadly since the Ayatollah Khomeini issued his infamous 'Fatwa' calling for the death of Salman Rushdie this respectable legal term has acquired an entirely negative connotation in the West and the mass media

6 www.onelawforall.org, www.no2sharia.org.uk http://www.secularism.org.uk/onelawforallcampaignlaunch eswith.html

Mediation is the classic ADR procedure and its purpose is to see if a legal dispute can be resolved by negotiation between the parties. The crucial point about mediation is that, even though most mediators are trained lawyers, mediation does not rely upon the application of legal rules or the determination of legal rights or wrongs it aims instead at finding common ground between parties and a solution they can both live with. (See www.civilmediation.org for further analysis.)

Arbitration by contrast is merely another form of trial before a 'judge' who is not appointed by the state but is instead agreed to by the parties. Arbitration is especially used in business disputes usually in order to ensure that the 'judge' has specialist knowledge of the area of business in question (in building contracts for example there is invariably an arbitration clause providing for the appointment of an arbitrator who is either a qualified surveyor or architect), or arbitration is chosen in order to maintain business confidentiality since arbitration hearings are not open to the public.

It is important to note that mediation and arbitration are not merely different in their philosophical basis but also different in their legal operation. Mediation may result in an agreement which can be subsequently presented to a court and registered as a legal decision but a mediator cannot impose a mediation decision and should not give directions or express opinions on legal issues or likelihoods of success. Mediation therefore leads to an agreement rather than a judgement and it is not, as such, regulated by statute.

More pertinently, a mediation agreement only has legal effect if it is ratified by a court which has to be satisfied that it is indeed an agreement between two parties who understand the legal consequences of what they have agreed to.

Arbitration, by contrast, is regulated by statute and involves the parties signing an arbitration agreement before the 'trial' begins. The arbitrator can act in accordance with the rules of any legal system specified in the arbitration agreement including, of course, sharia law and the ultimate 'judgement' of the arbitrator can be registered with the civil courts and enforced in the same way as if it were a judgement of the ordinary civil courts. It is this aspect of civil courts enforcing arbitration judgements based on sharia principles which has led to suggestions that sharia law has been given 'official' recognition.

However it is important to understand that the Arbitration Act does not extend to all areas of law: it does not cover criminal disputes and it does not extend to divorce or childcare cases, which is where the problems arise with the views of the LCJ: 'there is no reason why principles of sharia law, or any other religious code, should not be the basis for mediation'. There is, in fact, every reason why the principles of sharia law should not be used as the basis for mediation and that is because mediation does not involve the application of legal rules, whether religious or otherwise, it involves a search for a mutually acceptable compromise. If MAT, or any other organisation, is applying shariah principles to a dispute, then it is engaged in arbitration not mediation and the two are not the same and should not be treated as if they were the same.

The MAT website in part seems to be holding itself out as a mediation organisation:

> A trial in a court necessarily involves a winner and a loser... This can be a disadvantage where there are reasons to maintain a good relationship after the verdict. An obvious example may include divorce and child custody cases... Court hearings impose a solution on the parties without their agreement and which may need to be enforced. If the parties are able to negotiate a resolution between them, to which they both agree, this should be less of a predicament.[7]

But a separate section of the website says:

> MAT will therefore, for the first time, offer the Muslim community a real and true opportunity to settle disputes in accordance with Islamic Sacred Law.[8]

Judging from its rules of procedure as set out on its website, MAT does not appear to distinguish between offering an arbitration service and offering mediation.[9]

The practical effects of this confusion could be very important in the area of family and childcare cases which is the area where both the Archbishop and the LCJ saw sharia as having a role to play. In the case of divorce, one of the main decisions a Family Court has

---

7   http://www.matribunal.com/alt_dispute_res.html

8   http://www.matribunal.com/index.html

9   http://www.matribunal.com/procedure_rules.html

to decide is the custody and care of any children, and such decisions have to be made by the court on the basis of an assessment of what is the 'interests of the child'. Since children share their parents and, since it is usually in a child's interests to keep in contact with both parents, mediation fills an important and valuable role in helping divorcees to reach custody and contact arrangements which they can both accept. In reaching such a mediated agreement there is no doubt that religious principles can be important in appealing to the parents' better nature and leading them to look at their responsibilities as parents rather than concentrating on their own negative feelings towards their former partner; however that is not the same as applying sharia law rules relating to child custody even if those sharia rules are regarded as 'sacred'.

Sharia law rules on child custody can be quite cut and dried and were indeed described by judges in the House of Lords as 'arbitrary and discriminatory' in the case of M (Lebanon) *v* Home Secretary ([2008] UKHL 64). In general, under sharia law custody of a child over seven years of age is given to the father, so what is a Family Court judge to do if presented with a 'mediation agreement' brokered by the MAT which gives custody of the children to the father? If it truly is a mediated agreement between the two parties deciding what is in the best interests of the child then in normal circumstances the court would register it and enforce it. However, the question is whether it really is a 'mediated' agreement or does it involve acquiescence by the woman in a sharia law rule which does not explicitly consider the interests of the child.

If it is acquiescence in a sharia law rule as opposed to a properly mediated settlement, then the Family Court cannot accept the 'mediation' agreement because it is not truly a mediation agreement and because enforcement of such a sharia judgement would be contrary to s6(1) of the Human Rights Act 1998. Under s6(1) 'It is unlawful for a public authority [which includes a Court] to act in a way which is incompatible with a Convention right', i.e. a right under the European Convention on Human Rights, and in the case of Refah Partisi *v* Turkey BAILII ([2003] ECHR 87) the European Court of Human Rights stated:

> Sharia, which faithfully reflects the dogmas and divine rules laid down by religion, is stable and invariable... It is difficult to declare one's respect for democracy and human rights while at the same time supporting a regime based on sharia, which clearly diverges from Convention values, particularly with regard to its criminal law and criminal procedure, its rules on the legal status of women and the way it intervenes in all spheres of private and public life in accordance with religious precepts.

Similarly in M (Lebanon) the House of Lords decided that shariah law rules on child custody were incompatible with the human rights protected by the Convention.

While freely chosen arbitration between equal parties in limited areas of law is long established in Britain, the attempt to extend sharia arbitration to family disputes under the misleading title of 'mediation' is a potential misuse of both arbitration and family law. In fairness to both MAT and the tabloid press, if the Lord Chief Justice can get the two concepts of mediation and arbitration horribly confused in his speech, then a lawyer, such as myself, can hardly blame the Archbishop of Canterbury, MAT or the press for being equally confused.

Neil Addison

Editor's Introduction

Should we allow sharia law to exist alongside British law? Most British people would answer this question with a resounding 'no'. It's not just that many requirements of sharia law are incompatible with our own laws. That would be bad enough. The reason for the justified and spontaneous outrage that followed the Archbishop of Canterbury's call for the recognition of sharia law in 2008 was that many people intuitively felt that equality under the law is the bedrock of Western civilisation. Take it away and you disrupt the whole edifice.

The ideal of 'one law for all' is the basic allegiance on which liberal-democratic nations rely. We can best understand our situation by comparison with earlier forms of loyalty. During most of human history people have tended to live in groups whose cohesiveness rested on conformity to established custom and practice. Individuals who did not conform could be exiled or killed. Liberalism is very different. It is not based on the conformity of every individual to the established social conventions of the day, but rather on respect for the unique personal qualities of each individual and the potential for advance that lies within each of us. But liberalism is not anarchism. It is a system of fixed rules laying down when compulsion will be applied and otherwise leaving people free to act according to their conscience. It aims to create a sphere of freedom for each person to develop personally and add their own contribution to the improvement of human societies. It does not naively assume that nothing but good will follow. On the contrary, a feature of any liberal society is that laws need to be constantly refined to reduce the harm caused by wrongful conduct. But the aim of law is always to set people free. In non-liberal systems such as sharia law, the aim is to control behaviour and to secure compliance.

Liberalism makes possible, not only personal development of skills, talents or moral and intellectual qualities, but also creates the space in which individuals can join groups and lead very different lives, including lives guided by religious faith. Modern liberalism emerged as a result of religious conflict and was intended as a solution to it. Loyalty to law allows us to respect each other despite differences. Above all, it makes it possible for strangers to get along with each other because, despite our natural tendency to fear or suspect the unknown, law creates certainties we can count on. Anything that undermines our faith in the law threatens the vital spirit that prevents liberal-democracy from disintegrating into a feud between factions.

Sharia law has already become quite entrenched in Britain. The Muslim Arbitration Tribunal[1] claims to deal with family, inheritance, mosque and commercial disputes and has courts in London, Birmingham,

---

1 See:
   http://www.timesonline.co.uk/tol/news/uk/crime/article4749
   183.ece

Bradford, Nuneaton and Manchester. In truth there are many more courts.

The home page of the website of the Muslim Arbitration Tribunal (MAT) goes out of its way to look official. It has a photograph of Lord Phillips of Worth Matravers when he was Lord Chief Justice (from 2005 to 2008) in his wig and finery. A bold heading declares 'Lord Chief Justice endorses ADR [alternative dispute resolution] under Shariah Law'.[2] Underneath it has a picture of Lord Hunt, a Government minister, who had announced his support for the MAT initiative on forced marriages. The website emphasises that MAT rulings are binding under English law:

> MAT will operate within the legal framework of England and Wales thereby ensuring that any determination reached by MAT can be enforced through existing means of enforcement open to normal litigants. Although MAT must operate within the legal framework of England and Wales, this does not prevent or impede MAT from ensuring that all determinations reached by it are in accordance with one of the recognised Schools of Islamic Sacred Law. MAT will therefore, for the first time, offer the Muslim community a real and true opportunity to settle disputes in accordance with Islamic Sacred Law with the knowledge that the outcome as determined by MAT will be binding and enforceable.

In October 2008 a Government minister in a written Parliamentary answer gave sharia courts a bigger

---

2   See:
    http://www.judiciary.gov.uk/docs/speeches/lcj_equality_bef
    ore_the_law_030708.pdf

Government seal of approval than ever before. Bridget Prentice, Parliamentary Under-Secretary of State in the Ministry of Justice, was careful to say that the Government does not 'accommodate' any religious legal systems, but she confirmed two developments. First that sharia courts are operating under the 1996 Arbitration Act, which allows private disputes to be settled by an independent arbitrator. And second that sharia rulings on family matters (that are not covered by arbitration) could be given the authority of a British court by seeking 'a consent order embodying the terms' of the sharia court ruling.

There are three concerns about sharia courts that purport to be systems of arbitration. First, voluntary arbitration is only acceptable if both parties genuinely consent. There is a good deal of intimidation of women in Muslim communities and the genuine consent of women could not be accepted as a reality. Second, women are not equal in sharia law. The Koran calls for witnesses in legal cases and says that if a male witness cannot be found two women will do. Effectively the voice of a woman is half that of a man. Third, religious guidance is effective because individuals fear God or wish to remain in good standing with fellow believers. In our legal system no punishments can be applied to individuals who fail to live up to religious require-ments other than the social pressure of disapproval. The pressure we exert when we express our disapproval of other members of a church or any voluntary association is unavoidable and an accepted part of life within a liberal society so long as we are

4

free to leave any association that goes too far. Under most interpretations of Islam a person who leaves the faith is an apostate who can be put to death. While this threat remains, it cannot be accepted that sharia councils are nothing more than independent arbitrators guided by faith. The reality is that for many Muslims, sharia courts are in practice part of an institutionalised atmosphere of intimidation, backed by the ultimate sanction of a death threat.

The underlying problem is that sharia law reflects male-dominated Asian and Arabic cultures. It cannot therefore be accepted as a legally valid basis even for settling private disagreements in a country like ours, where our law embodies the equal legal status of everyone, regardless of race, gender or religion. Our system is based on moral and legal equality or it is nothing. Moreover, further encouragement of sharia law, far from helping integration, will undermine the efforts of British Muslims struggling to evolve a version of Islam consistent with a tolerant and pluralistic society.

A great battle is being fought between rival groups for the support of fellow Muslims. We have become familiar with the groups who direct their hatred against Western civilisation, but the most numerous are fundamentalist rather than violent. Their aim is to prevent Muslims who live in the West from falling under the influence of Christianity or secular liberalism. The leaders of fundamentalist factions want Muslims to owe their allegiance to their particular interpretation of Islam, whether it be Wahhabi, Salafi, or any of the countless other doctrines whose adherents are convinced of their own righteousness. For them, loyalty to any national system of liberal-democratic government is no more than a rival for the affections of followers. Freedom of conscience is not in their vocabulary. Such leaders are accustomed to living in Muslim countries where the powers of government can be used to enforce compliance and they plan to use British law to coerce Muslims into leading lives separate from the British liberal mainstream. If we permit the growing intrusion of sharia courts to continue, British Muslims will in effect be subject to the same coercive pressures to conform as they would in an Asian village. Liberalism has always been tolerant of a plurality of lifestyles, but only if they are freely chosen.

A similar controversy came to a head in the Canadian province of Ontario in 2005. The province had passed an Arbitration Act in 1991 to allow disputes to be settled by legally binding arbitration, including disputes based on religious principles. The system initially became controversial in 2003 when the formation of the Islamic Institute of Civil Justice was founded to offer arbitration in family and other disputes in accordance with sharia law. In December 2004 a former Canadian attorney general, Marion Boyd, produced an official report for the Ontario Government and recommended in favour of arbitration according to Islamic law. A furious debate followed led by Muslim women who argued that they had gone to Canada to get away from sharia law and the coercion that it embodied. In September 2005 the premier of Ontario announced that the Arbitration Act would be amended to ensure 'one law for all'. The amendment was passed in February 2006, effectively ending religious-based arbitration.

There is another dimension to the controversy that has so far received scant attention, as the distinguished barrister Neil Addison points out in his Foreword— namely the tendency to confuse mediation and arbitration. Mediation under religious supervision, when both parties genuinely seek moral guidance from their faith, will often be an admirable process that will help disputing individuals to overcome their selfish instincts. And given that mediation is not enforceable, it is less open to abuse by elements who seek to intimidate weaker parties. However, no religion should have the power to use force against its adherents. Arbitration entails legal compulsion and consequently nothing less will suffice than the exclusion of sharia courts from recognition under Britain's Arbitration Act of 1996. The approach taken in Ontario is one possibility. In that state, family arbitrations were required to be conducted exclusively under Canadian law. Ontario's 2006 amendment had the effect of barring enforcement of family arbitrations under both religious laws and the laws of other countries. Family dispute resolution processes carried out under rules other than Canadian law were not prohibited, but they had no legal effect from 2006.

'One law for all' is the principle that should guide our lawmakers, but as in so many other respects in recent years Parliament has lost its way. Denis MacEoin's study is an excellent introduction to the issues at stake and his revelations about some of the 'case law' are alarming.

David G. Green

Sharia Law or 'One Law For All'?

Denis MacEoin

Islam, like Judaism, is a religion of the law. Sharia law, honed over many centuries, is a distillation of rulings that purport to represent the divine diktat in all worldly affairs. There is little in personal or public life that it does not touch. In this respect, it differs from the Jewish *halakha* in one major way: it provides injunctions for the conduct of criminal, public and even international law. It is best known in the West for the more barbaric of these rulings, from the stoning of adulterers and the amputation of the hands of thieves to the proclamation of holy war and the declaration of truces.

Outside the Muslim world, where sharia often still holds sway, even in countries with codified secular legislation, it is restricted to ritual, personal and family matters. Rulings on prayer, fasting, the payment of alms to the poor and related religious duties are, by their very nature, uncontroversial: they seldom if ever come within the purview of the non-Muslim state. (One of the few instances in recent times was the occupation of the road outside the East London mosque by radical preacher Abu Hamza and his followers, where the thoroughfare was devoted exclusively to Friday prayers.) But family law threatens to cross or actually does cross the threshold between the personal and public realms. Laws concerning marriage and divorce, the custody of children, the payment of alimony, the treatment of sexual impropriety and much else all bring with them great potential for controversy or the commission of acts that may run counter to UK legal norms or human rights legislation. In some cases they have been and are used as an excuse for bigotry towards homosexuals, Muslims who have abandoned their faith, non-Muslims in general or members of the public who have been deemed to criticise or mock Islam. In the Netherlands, film director Theo van Gogh was killed by a young fanatic who believed he was acting according to sharia principles.[1]

In recent years, there have been several calls for parliament to acknowledge a limited code of sharia law as a parallel system within the UK, allowing Muslims to manage their personal and family affairs according to the demands of the Qur'an, its ancillary texts, and the body of jurisprudence that has been built up by Muslim scholars down many generations. In August

1   At his trial in June 2005, Van Gogh's killer, Mohammed Bouyeri, declared 'I did what I did purely out of my beliefs. I want you to know that I acted out of conviction and not that I took his life because he was Dutch or because I was Moroccan and felt insulted.' He had previously started to live by strict Islamic rules, and may have been inspired by the Imam Fawaz of the al-Sunnah Mosque in The Hague, who declared in a sermon that Van Gogh was a criminal. See Anthony Browne, 'Muslim radical confesses to Van Gogh killing in court tirade', *The Times*, 12 June 2005, available at: http://www.timesonline.co.uk/tol/news/world/article543212.ece

2006, the head of the Union of Muslim Organisations of the UK and Ireland, Dr Sayed Pasha, called on Ruth Kelly, then Secretary of State for Communities, to institute public holidays to mark Muslim festivals (something that has never been done for any other religious group) and to introduce elements of sharia law to cover family matters.[2] These calls have generally been made by Muslim groups and individuals, but, as is well known, it was only in February 2008 that the Archbishop of Canterbury, Rowan Williams, joined his voice to theirs in a plea for the limited application of Islamic law within the United Kingdom.[3]

The present report seeks to present the case for a denial of the broadened use of sharia, arguing that it is inappropriate to this country for reasons that are not prejudicial of Islam per se or critical of Muslims as such, but are, rather, linked to elements in Islamic law that are seriously out of step with trends in Western legislation that derive from the values of the Enlightenment and are inherent in modern codes of human rights that are in force throughout Europe and in democratic countries elsewhere. Further objections derive from a majority of Muslims in the UK (and very

---

2   Colin Brown, *Independent*, 15 August 2006, available at: http://www.independent.co.uk/news/uk/politics/let-us-adopt-islamic-family-law-to-curb-extremists-muslims-tell-kelly-411954.html

3   For the full text of Williams's speech, go to: http://www.archbishopofcanterbury.org/1575

likely elsewhere too), who reject the introduction of sharia in general or for specific matters.

In 2007, the think tank Policy Exchange published a detailed poll of Muslim opinion that covered most issues relevant to the position of the community in modern Britain. Examining cultural attitudes, the researchers asked the question: 'If I could choose, I would prefer to live in Britain under sharia law rather than British law'. Respondents gave different answers according to age groups, but there was a broad consensus that sharia was unsuited to the UK: 75 per cent of those over 55 preferred British law, though this figure went down as ages dropped: 75 per cent of 45-54 year-olds, 63 per cent of 35-44 year-olds, 52 per cent of 25-34 year-olds, and only 50 per cent of 16-24 year-olds.[4] This reflects a trend towards extremism on the part of young Muslims in general.

The same poll posed a more differentiated question: 'The following is a list of laws that are defined in most scholarly interpretations of sharia law. Please say if you personally agree or disagree with the law mentioned'. The responses to these questions were not as encouraging as those to the broader one:[5]

4   Munira Mirza, Abi Senthilkumaran, and Zein Ja'far, *Living apart together: British Muslims and the paradox of multiculturalism*, London: Policy Exchange, 2007, p. 46. Many of the figures given below do not add up. I have reprinted them as they stand in the text.

5   Munira Mirza, Abi Senthilkumaran, and Zein Ja'far, *Living apart together*, p. 47.

'That a Muslim woman may not marry a non-Muslim'

Age group	Agreed (%)	Disagreed (%)	Did not know (%)
55+	42	43	14
45-54	40	54	6
35-44	50	45	6
25-34	55	40	4
16-24	56	40	4

Overall, a majority of 51 per cent agreed

'That a Muslim woman cannot marry without the consent of her guardian'

Age group	Agreed (%)	Disagreed (%)	Did not know (%)
55+	33	56	11
45-54	25	67	6
35-44	39	56	5
25-34	47	48	5
16-24	57	41	2

Overall, a majority of 51 per cent disagreed

'That a Muslim male may have up to four wives, and a Muslim female is allowed only one husband'

Age group	Agreed (%)	Disagreed (%)	Did not know (%)
55+	18	74	8
45-54	38	52	9
35-44	44	52	3
25-34	52	42	7
16-24	52	43	5

Overall 48 per cent disagreed

'That Muslim conversion is forbidden and punishable by death'

Age group	Agreed (%)	Disagreed (%)	Did not know (%)
55+	19	74	8
45-54	19	68	11
35-44	27	58	14
25-34	37	50	10
16-24	36	57	7

Overall, a majority of 57 per cent disagreed

'That homosexuality is wrong and should be illegal'

Age group	Agreed (%)	Disagreed (%)	Did not know (%)
55+	50	39	11
45-54*	54	36	9
35-44	55	36	9
25-34	65	26	8
16-24	71	24	6

* 1% is missing

Overall, a large majority of 61 per cent agreed

Policy Exchange went further and asked whether their respondents would agree to reform of sharia law. They asked the following question:

> Some Islamic scholars have called for a major reinter-pretation of sharia law to reflect modern ideas about human rights, equality for women and tolerance of religious conversion. Other Islamic scholars disagree with this view and say that sharia law is absolute and should not be

interpreted to fit in with Western values. Which of these is closest to your opinion?

Here are the responses:

Age group	Pro-reform (%)	Against (%)	Did not know (%)
55+	57	32	1
45-54	56	30	21
35-44	49	36	16
25-34	49	44	19
16-24	37	42	9

Overall, 49 per cent favoured reform; 39 per cent were against it; and 16 per cent did not know

The above figures are both encouraging and discouraging. A majority of Muslims reject the idea of living in Britain under sharia law; a majority would allow a woman to marry without the consent of a male guardian; a majority disagree that conversion is forbidden and punishable by death; and almost half would opt for re-interpretation of sharia in a reformist direction.

But some of these majorities are marginal. And there are majorities that clash with British cultural values: 51 per cent agree that a Muslim woman may not marry a non-Muslim, 61 per cent think homo-sexuality should be made illegal. Although they are in a minority, those opposed to reform of the sharia make up a hefty 39 per cent. More importantly, there is a visible trend from greater tolerance among the older age groups to an increase in hardline attitudes among young people, particularly the 16-20 year-old age band.

Fully 37 per cent of 16-24 year-olds prefer sharia, 56 per cent agree that a Muslim woman must not marry a non-Muslim, 57 per cent agree that a Muslim woman cannot marry without consent of her guardian, 52 per cent agree that a man may have up to four wives, a woman only one husband, and 71 per cent agree homosexuality should be made illegal.

Some of the questions are not well phrased. It would be interesting to know what the responses would have been had pollsters asked whether conversion was forbidden, without adding 'and punishable with death', or whether homosexuality was wrong, without adding 'and should be illegal'.

A similarly wide-ranging survey carried out in the previous year by GfK NOP Social Research for Channel 4 Dispatches, *Attitudes to Living in Britain—A Survey of Muslim Opinion*, reached similar conclusions.[6] Of 1,000 Muslims surveyed, 30 per cent said they preferred sharia law (34 per cent among 18-24 year-olds).[7] If we extrapolate from this figure, assuming recent figures of two million Muslims living in the UK,[8] we may calculate that some 600,000 Muslims would prefer to live in Britain under sharia law. A not insignificant

---

6   Dated 27 April 2006. Available online in pdf form at: http://www.imaginate.uk.com/MCC01_SURVEY/Site%20Download.pdf

7   *Attitudes*, p. 16.

8   See Travis, Alan, 'Officials think UK's Muslim population has risen to 2m', *Guardian*, 8 April 2008.

number—19 per cent—said further that they would willingly move to a country ruled by sharia; but this figure went up hugely to 46 per cent of those who said they preferred sharia.[9]

A variation on this is a desire on the part of 28 per cent for Britain to become an Islamic state. This may be unrealistic, but it undoubtedly forms intentions, especially among those who favour sharia, 45 per cent of whom expressed this hope.[10]

Attitudes towards sharia exercise a marked effect on a range of other positions. For example, while a shamefully low percentage overall (34 per cent) agreed that the Holocaust had really happened (meaning some 60 per cent believed it had not), only 19 per cent of those who preferred sharia said it had taken place.[11] If this is worrying, it is also a matter for concern that a full 23 per cent of those who prefer sharia said they would not vote in elections.[12] Twenty-six per cent of those who favour sharia said they would withdraw their daughter from school rather than send her without *hijab*, and an equal 26 per cent said they would just send her wearing *hijab* anyway.[13]

---

9   *Attitudes*, p. 17.

10   *Attitudes*, p.18.

11   *Attitudes*, p. 28.

12   *Attitudes*, p. 42

13   *Attitudes*, p. 44.

Two final figures are even more worrying. A full 62 per cent of sharia-minded Muslims argued that there is no truth at all in the statement 'How much truth is there in the idea that Islam treats women as second-class citizens'.[14] And an even larger number (71 per cent) agreed that wives should always obey their husbands.[15] These last two attitudes are of particular importance, given that the bulk of the work done by courts relates to areas that have a profound bearing on the status and freedom of Muslim women.

Let's take a closer look at sharia law itself, at the sources from which it is derived, the four schools that shape it, the areas it covers, and the characteristics of Muslim family law.

Sources

Sharia law is generally held to be formed from four sources. These were formulated in the first centuries of Islam and have held true down to the present day. The first thing the reader should notice is that it is a gross oversimplification to speak of Islamic law as 'Qur'anic law'. It is that, yet much more.

The four sources are: the Qur'an, the sunna (i.e. the sayings and doings of the Prophet and his companions), consensus (in theory of the community, in practice that of legal scholars, the ulema), and analogical reasoning (i.e. 'if the law says such and such

14 *Attitudes*, p. 45.

15 *Attitudes*, p. 47.

in one instance, ought it not to say the same in another?'). Over the centuries, there has been little or no deviation from the rulings derived from these sources. 'Little was lost from the tradition, even when it became irrelevant to real life.'[16]

The Qur'an

At the heart of all Islamic law in all places and periods stands the holy book, the Qur'an. In order to appreciate the impact of this singular book on the development of sharia and the force it still exerts in the modern era, we need to know just how the sacred text is understood and how it is applied by a majority of Muslims.

The holy book is not particularly long, nor is it coherent or systematic. Every word is deemed to be the direct word of God, and the whole text is a perfect replica of a tablet in heaven. Historically, the book is a record of what was 'sent down' to the prophet Muhammad over a period of 22 years, between his first moment of revelation in the year 610 to his death in 632. Muslims do not consider it to be the words of Muhammad, however (though most non-Muslim scholars would, of course, argue that it cannot be anything else).

The text is fixed and unchangeable, with remarkably little evidence for early recensions. Its unchangeability is

---

16 Calder, Norman, 'Legal Thought and Jurisprudence', in Esposito, John (ed.), *The Oxford Encyclopedia of Islam in the Modern World*, New York and Oxford, 1995, vol. 2, p. 452.

a doctrinal absolute: tradition records that the Qur'an originally existed co-eternally with God in heaven. It was only in Muhammad's lifetime that the archangel Gabriel was sent to earth to convey to the prophet, a little at a time, verses taken from the heavenly original. Muhammad in turn recited these verses, thereby passing them on to his followers. It was (tradition states) only a few years after the prophet's death, in the reign of the Caliph Uthman (d. 656), that the first collection of the text was made from scattered fragments. What we have in our hands today is a confused re-ordering of these 'revealed' verses, organised on a simple basis of longest first, shortest last, with no reference to chronology. Later, a need grew to identify *suras* and verses according to the time and circumstances in which they were first uttered. This became vitally important when it came to the configuration of the sharia system, as we shall see.

The Qur'an is not in any proper sense a book of laws, and it is better not to think of it as such. It contains homilies, fragmented Biblical narratives, occasional historical details, exhortations, recriminations, injunctions to fight holy war, meditations on nature, discourses on peoples of the past and their fate, reflections on God... and some legal rulings. Many of these rulings are cast in unclear or ambiguous language and thus are subject to interpretation by later generations. For example, sura 4 verse 3 says that a man may marry up to four wives, but qualifies this by pointing out that fairness demands that he only marry one (or take a concubine): some take this as a green light for anyone who thinks he can treat more than one woman with fairness to marry two or more; more recently, it has been used (in conjunction with another verse [sura 4:129], *'It is not within your power to be perfectly equitable in your treatment with all your wives, even if you wish to be so'*) as grounds for instituting monogamy.

But it is the lack of evident chronology in the text that puts most Qur'anic legislation in need of a different sort of interpretation. Anyone who reads the book will be struck by its not infrequent contradictions. Famously, there are early verses that enjoin a positive attitude towards Jews and Christians;[17] and there are other, later ones, that caution Muslims against taking such unbelievers as friends, that demonise them, and that permit the fighting of holy war against them.

How does a Muslim know what to believe? One reading leads to friendship and good community relations, the other to perpetual hatred and the creation of ghettos. The answer is a doctrine called 'abrogated and abrogating verses', which determines that early verses are abrogated by later ones. It is these latter verses that are generally thought to carry force today. Of course, establishing which verses are early and which late was never an easy task, but it was accomplished in the early centuries to most people's

---

17 Termed People of the Book because they have received divine scriptures (which they subsequently corrupted).

satisfaction.[18] This presents a problem, however. There are two broad periods into which the Qur'an is traditionally divided: that of Mecca, which ended in 622 when the Prophet and his companions decamped for the city of Medina, and a second period covering the ten years he lived in Medina. Meccan verses account for a more literal and eirenic attitude on Muhammad's part, much influenced by his favourable attitude to the Jews of the region; Medinan verses display a more legalistic and harsh outlook, to a great degree inspired by the Prophet's bitterness on finding that the Jews had no wish to convert to Islam.

Used by conservatives, the principle of abrogation can be used to block attempts by would-be reformers to bring Qur'anic teaching in line with modern needs and attitudes.[19] Whatever happens in the years to come, the Qur'an will remain central to each and every debate that takes place about Islamic law, whether in the West or in the Muslim world.

2. *Sunna*

The Qur'an is far from providing a complete legal system capable of catering for the widening needs of

---

18 It was, of course, never carried out using the tools of modern textual scholarship and linguistic analysis.

19 For examples of modern Muslim thinkers who have experimented with Western techniques of interpretation, see Suha Taji-Farouki (ed.), *Modern Muslim Intellectuals and the Qur 'an*, Oxford, OUP, 2004.

Islamic society. This was true as far back as the earliest days of Islam. Clearly, the fragmentary legal verses of the Book had to be supplemented. Naturally, the first Muslims looked for this supplementation to the life of Muhammad, especially as lived in Medina, where he had been the effective governor or prince of a mini-state, and where his encounters with others had provided models on which legal rulings might be based. People wanted to know how the Prophet had passed legal judgements, what sort of questions his companions had asked him, what sort of answers they had received, and how they had behaved in reference to what they had seen Muhammad do or what they had once heard him say. This prophetic example came to be known as the *sunna*. Its relationship to the Qur'an is crucial to how the sharia is understood: according to the eighth-century jurisprudent Abu Amr Abd al-Rahman al-Awzai, the Book is in greater need of the sunna than the sunna of the Book.[20]

In order to fill this broad gap, two related bodies of information emerged in the first Islamic centuries: biographies of the Prophet and collections of his sayings and doings. These latter, generally known as Traditions (*hadith*, pl. *ahadith*) enjoy a sacralised quality that puts them next to the Qur'an in authority, though the words of Muhammad are in no way considered the word of God. However, the Qur'an itself describes

---

20 Narrated by al-Darimi and others and cited by Ibn 'Abd al-Barr in *Jami ' Bayan al- 'Ilm* (2:1193-1194 #2351); and al-Shatibi in *al-Muwafaqat* (Salafiyya ed. 1343 4:10).

Muhammad as a 'model' for his followers, and this gives to the tiniest detail of his way of life a sense of permanent significance. These details together make up the *sunna*.

Sunni collections refer to Traditions that have been collected into six canonical compilations, of which two extensive texts stand out as the most authentic: The 'Authentic Collection' of Muhammad al-Bukhari (d.870) and the 'Authentic Collection' of his contemporary, Muslim ibn al-Hajjaj (d.874). The Shia have their own collections and also rely on the sayings and doings of their holy imams.

Since the Traditions are much more detailed than the Qur'an, their richness of incident makes up extremely well for their subordinate status. In the modern period they have acquired fresh importance in the eyes of a new breed of fundamentalists, broadly termed Salafis. The Salaf (after whom they are named) were the first three generations of Muslims—the Prophet and his companions, their sons, and their grandchildren. In a desire for religious purity and in the hope of avoiding innovation in the faith, Salafis reject later jurisprudence and concentrate on the Qur'an and Traditions, supplemented only by the Prophetic biographies.

It is worth adding here that innovation (*bida*) is widely considered a form of heresy or outright unbelief. The Prophet is recorded as saying: 'Every new matter is an innovation, every innovation is mis-guidance, and every misguidance is in the Fire' [of

Hell].[21] Few things have damaged Islam as much as this doctrine. It has had a severe dampening effect on attempts at legal reform, above all in the modern period, when most Muslims live in a world characterised by technical, scientific, legal, political and social innovation. At its worst, as in the case of Wahhabis and Salafis, this can lead to an insistence on a return to the state of law that is supposed to have existed in the time of the Prophet and his companions. By thus idealising a perfect state of government and legislation, it becomes all too easy to dismiss or condemn anything that does not match up to these impossible standards.

The term *sunna* is widely used to describe matters that are deemed to be properly Islamic, to be traditionally sound, because they are based on the way of the Prophet. In spite of this, it has a looser usage. It often refers, for example, to the practices of clitoridectomy or full female genital mutilation (fgm),[22] which actually have only a marginal existence in the hadith literature. Their persistence contradicts their condemnation as unIslamic by many Muslim authorities, including the shaykh of al-Azhar University in Cairo, Muhammad

---

21 Hadith from al-Nasa' i, *al-Sunan al-sughra*.

22 On the incidence of fgm and attitudes towards it, see Brandon, J. and Hafez, S., *Crimes of the Community: Honour-based violence in the UK*, London: Centre for Social Cohesion, 2008, p. 65 ff. For some Muslim rulings, see 'Debates about FGM in Africa, the Middle East and the Far East', at: http://www.religioustolerance.org/fem_cirm.htm

Sayyid Tantawi, the leading authority in the Sunni world.[23]

Consensus

Traditionally, this has been understood as the consensus of religious scholars, the ulema, even though some modern thinkers extend it to all believers. It has its roots in a saying of the Prophet that 'My community will not agree on an error'. The restriction of consensus to the clergy (which is normative even today) means that a sharp division is created between the 'learned' and all other Muslims. The unlearned are not equipped with the specialised knowledge that would allow them to understand and participate in legal matters. This division is particularly marked in Shiism, where there is a more defined clerical hierarchy than in Sunnism.

In recent years, the learned class has come to be more emphasised, especially in traditionalist and fundamentalist circles. A rapid increase in the number of theological/jurisprudential seminaries in many countries (the UK included) has ensured a steady flow of radicalised clergy. These institutions are often funded by or are based in Saudi Arabia, while others are attached to the North Indian/Pakistani Deobandi movement. The latter includes a circle of seminaries in this country, centred on the Darul Uloom at Bury.

---

23 'Egyptian ban on female circumcision upheld', BBC News at: http://news.bbc.co.uk/2/hi/42914.stm

These home-grown clerics are generally more rigorous than the imams from the sub-continent, who previously dominated the British scene.

Analogical Reasoning

This is simply a means for extending existing rulings to fresh situations while avoiding innovation. If we assume that wine is prohibited because of its intoxicating qualities and because intoxication clouds the mind, diverting it from its proper focus on God, prayer, etc., then it follows that marijuana must also be forbidden, for the same reason.

In Islam, as in Judaism, considerable effort is needed to master the texts and techniques needed to follow and make legal rulings. Among the large number of learned clergy, the most significant are the jurisprudents (*fuqaha*), who specialise in sharia. Those who possess all the necessary textual and rational skills to do so can acquire the status of Mufti (literally, someone who issues fatwas). A fatwa is simply a ruling on a matter of sharia law, usually issued in reply to a question framed by some member of the public. The fashioning of such rulings forms the basis for the work of sharia courts. These rulings are often collected and published, often in Arabic, but increasingly in English. They appear on numerous websites, such as Ask Imam or IslamOnline, and are available to sharia courts, where they are chosen on the strength of the original mufti who issued them, or the validity of his religious affiliation.

The Four Schools of Law

To the outsider, Islam may at first appear monolithic; but a closer look reveals something quite different. Islam knows no major divisions apart from the very unbalanced Sunni-Shi'i split.[24] Nevertheless, a range of local, regional and international versions of the faith create a multi-dimensional reality that often has a direct bearing on how the law is conceived and administered. There are, to begin with, great variations in practice from country to country or region to region. Moroccan Islam is quite distinct from the Indonesian variety, while Indonesian differs from Pakistani, Pakistani from Turkish, and so on. These variations combine local traditions with a range of allegiances, including the different law schools of the Sunni world. It is quite normal to find local customs, some of them pre-Islamic, jostling for space alongside the more formal Islam of the ulema.

There is a persistent gulf between the numerous Sufi orders, with their stress on mysticism and the cult of saints, centred on local tombs, and the strictly puritan

---

24 It is generally reckoned that Shi'i Muslims constitute only ten per cent of the total Muslim population, around 132,000,000 people. For a good breakdown of overall statistics, go to:
http://www.umaamerica.org/magazine2005/magazine_article_shiainworld.asp

style of Wahhabis, Salafis and other fundamentalists.[25] Yet Sufis fight in jihad and serve as judges, imams or even as ulema. There are Sunni Sufis and Shi'i Sufis, sober Sufis and ecstatic Sufis. The great Pakistani division between Barelwis and Deobandis is not as sharp as it may appear, given that both sides follow Sufi orders. This is not irrelevant to our discussion: such differences and similarities exert a great influence on the degree of emphasis placed by one group or another on the law in general, or on local tradition within a national community.

Much of the current trend towards a puritan style of legalism comes from controversial fundamentalist groups like the Wahhabis of Saudi Arabia (who exercise a global influence through the use of oil money), the Muslim Brotherhood, the more diffuse Salafis, and, in the UK, the dominant Indo-Pakistani movement of the Deobandis.

Across the regions, Sunnis are divided by four traditional schools of law. These schools do not amount to separate churches or denominations, and there is no sectarian antagonism between them; but they do dictate ritual practice and legal opinion, and attachment is not on the whole by choice, but according to one's place of birth or residence.

---

25 A clear (if idealised) picture of how a Muslim radical moved from a hardline creed to Sufism is given in Husain, E., *The Islamist*, London, 2007.

The Hanafi School

The Hanafi school of law is named for Numan ibn Thabit Abu Hanifa, an Iranian who lived in the city of Kufa in what is now Iraq. He died there in 767, just over a century after the death of Muhammad; but he was born in 699, which meant he belonged to the generation that followed the Prophet's companions. This closeness to prophetic times adds to his lustre as a legal authority.

The school that he and other early scholars forged is today the most widespread in the Sunni world. Its adherents make up over one-third of Sunnis. It holds sway in matters of personal law throughout the Balkans, the Caucasus, Afghanistan, Pakistan, India, Central Asia, and western China (Xinjiang). Some significant groups who adhere to Hanafi law include the Deobandis and Barelwis (who are otherwise bitter rivals), the Tablighi Jamaat (a widespread Pakistani missionary movement that emerged from the Deobandis), and the Taleban (also a Deobandi off-shoot). The first three groups have a marked presence in the UK, where a majority of mosques are controlled by the Deobandis).

The Maliki School

This school takes its name from Malik ibn Anas, a scholar who lived in Medina from his birth in 713 to his death in 795. His school (which is strictly bound by Tradition), encapsulates the legal thought of the city in which the Prophet lived his last ten years, and where so many of his companions and their descendants continue to live. This 'living tradition' of Medina outweighed even the hadith being collected around this time. The school is conservative, especially in its attitude to women and its contempt for innovation. It is dominant in North Africa (except for Egypt) and has spread to Sudan, Bahrain, the Emirates and Kuwait.

The Shafii School

This is named after Muhammad ibn Idris al-Shafii (d. 820). Al-Shafii was the great systematiser of Islamic law, and his school brings together many earlier strands. It enjoys great popularity among a majority of Muslims in the Palestinian territories and Jordan, with large numbers in Syria, Lebanon, Iraq, the Hijaz (in Saudi Arabia), Pakistan, India and Indonesia.

The Hanbali School

The Hanbalis follow the principles laid down by Ahmad ibn Hanbal (d. 855). Ibn Hanbal lived in Baghdad, the new capital of the Abbasid empire, a city founded only 30 years before his birth. He travelled widely in search of traditions and legal rulings, and from this raw material and his own legal opinions and fatwas, his successors built up a body of juristic principles and laws. As a result, Hanbalis are the most hardline and conservative of the four schools, and their school has given birth to many fundamentalist and puritan teachers, including Taqi al-Din Ahmad ibn Taymiyya (d. 1327), whose work has inspired most modern Salafi thinkers, and Muhammad ibn Abd al-Wahhab (d. 1792), founder of the strict Wahhabi movement which underpins the puritan regime in modern Saudi Arabia, a primary source of religious rulings via a well-regulated and authoritative circle of religious councils and universities. Hanbali law is followed in Saudi Arabia and Qatar and has followers in the Palestinian territories, Syria, Iraq and elsewhere.

Islamic Law in Modern Times

As we have just seen, all the basic features of sharia law were laid down in the early centuries of the faith. The Hadith collections, the lives of the Prophet, the four main law schools, the principles of Qur'anic interpretation all took their basic shape within a short space of time. Common to all of them was the belief that innovation was bad and tradition was something that must be adhered to in almost all cases.

But it is a mistake to think there were no further developments in law or jurisprudence during the centuries that followed. New scholars and new cases, together with the impact of social reality in the many Islamic empires within which religious law had to work alongside customary law of one kind or another, all left their imprint on the body of the sharia as interpreted by the ulema and administered by state functionaries. Nevertheless, with the passage of time it became apparent that Islam was essentially conservative at heart and seldom open to fresh ideas or practices. There were—and are—several reasons for this. One is the inevitable conservatism of religions in general, since there will always be a focus on founding figures, sacred texts and an unrealistic belief that the past was better than the present. The shadow of a Golden Age in the days of the Prophet and his immediate successors lies heavily over the centuries that follow. Muslims are committed to preserve the way of the Prophet and his companions, none of whom may be criticised in the slightest way; to the utter impossibility of changing the text of Qur'an; and to a conviction that the first generations enjoyed and understood a purer form of the faith and should, therefore, be imitated down to the last detail, however little relevance this may have to the world in which they actually live.

From the Middle Ages, Muslim society remained largely static. Important things happened, of course, but the basic characteristics of Islamic culture remained fixed, partly because there was relatively little material change, and partly because religious conservatism acted as a brake on what change there might have been. The doctrine of innovation as heresy did much to dampen intellectual curiosity in areas like philosophy and science, even if great thinkers like Ibn al-Arabi or Mulla Sadra challenged the dry formulations of the clergy. Much intellectual effort went into the religious sciences of jurisprudence, Qur'an commentary and their various branches. For centuries, the only kind of higher education available to Muslims was that available in religious seminaries (*madrasas*).

Contact between Muslims and Europeans was sporadic. The Ottoman Turks had closer relations with the West than any previous empire, but even they retained intact most features of classical Islamic civilisation, borrowing European military techniques and equipment, but rejecting almost everything else, including the printing press.

But in the late eighteenth century relations with the West started to undergo a dramatic change. The distant and despised Christians, about whom the Muslim world remained remarkably ill-informed, entered the realms of Islam as conquerors. By the end of the nineteenth century, most Muslim countries were direct or indirect colonies of European powers. Even where unconquered (like Iran), they came under enormous pressure.[26]

This new contact exposed many Muslims to the continuing advances in Western science, agriculture, weaponry, education, shipping, trade and culture. It also opened up aspects of Western progress in areas like constitutional democracy, democratic freedoms, growing equality for women, the separation of church and state, secularism and codified legal systems with laws passed by parliaments. These latter presented advantages to a growing band of modernisers (above all in the Ottoman empire) who embraced such ideas and sought to implement them in their own countries.

---

26 On this general development, see Lewis, B., *What Went Wrong? Western Impact and Middle Eastern Response*, London, 2002.

In almost all countries, they met opposition from rulers who saw democracy as a threat and religious leaders who considered any change in the law as a direct challenge to Islam itself. In some places, changes were introduced by colonial administrations, in others by indigenous elites. Muslim students coming back from Europe often carried with them the gospel of social change and a zeal to catch up with the West.

Secular schools were opened alongside colleges of higher education where Turks, Iranians, Egyptians, Indians and others could learn engineering, biology or medicine. By the mid-twentieth century, as the imperial powers left their former colonies, country after country introduced its own civil code, usually incorporating Western legislation (mainly French) alongside a truncated body of sharia law.

None of this came easily, nor has the struggle between secular and religious law come to an end. From the beginning, the ulema saw two of their main power bases pulled from under them: education and jurisprudence. Later, some saw their professions and even their lives threatened as absolutist rulers like Ataturk or Reza Shah tried to drive through secularist reform by force.

Even where the religious establishment saw a need for reform, so wedded were the ulema to the past that they conceived of true reform as a return to the purity of prophetic times. The Egyptian reformer Muhammad Abduh (d. 1905) sought flexibility to adapt Islam to modern times, but stressed the importance of clearing away late ideas and returning to the time of the Salaf, the first three generations of the faith. His successor, Rashid Rida (d. 1935) intensified this emphasis on the Salaf, creating a powerful movement opposed to modernism of all kinds. Another Egyptian, Hasan al-Banna (d. 1949), the founder of the pervasive Muslim Brotherhood, advanced similar views and these were forcibly advanced by a later Brotherhood thinker, Sayyid Qutb (1966), the father of modern violent Islamism.

The Salafi premise is simple: Islam can only be reformed by cutting away the many accretions that have gathered to it over the centuries, dumping the four orthodox law schools, and cutting back to the two most reliable sources for faith, conduct, and religious law: the Qur'an and the Sunna. This largely matches an earlier formulation, that of the Wahhabi movement in what is now Saudi Arabia. Although the Saudi kingdom is officially Hanbali, the underlying drive is for legislation based on scriptural authority (as distinct from the accumulated rulings of the four law schools). The Islamic University of Medina, which attracts students from all round the world, was set up to accommodate Salafis. Many leading scholars in the West, including Britain, have studied there.

In general, the religious leadership has remained profoundly conservative, and this has prompted counter-reactions to even the most modest of reforms. In India in 1978, for example, a woman named Shah Bano petitioned the courts to secure maintenance from a husband who had divorced her previously. The case reached the Supreme Court seven years later. This court cited section 125 of the Indian Code of Criminal Procedure and ordered the husband to pay her alimony. The conservative forces erupted with indignation and forced the Prime Minister to accede to their demand that the court's ruling be overturned. In 1986, parliament passed the Muslim Women (Protection of Rights on Divorce) Act 1986, overruling the Supreme Court and upholding Muslim Penal Law. It is unlikely that India will in future create a common civil law code that discriminates against no-one on the grounds of religious affiliation. The involvement of the Islamic clergy in Indian politics (as in Pakistan and Bangladesh) has generally been a barrier to reform at all levels.

In recent years, there has been a wider trend in some countries to reject Western-style law codes in favour of sharia. This has happened in various degrees in Nigeria, Sudan, Somalia under the Islamic Courts Union, Iran and Afghanistan under the Taleban. Some countries have scarcely moved away from a sharia-based system, among them Saudi Arabia and the Gulf states. Bahrain's clergy have acquired much greater power since the 2006 move to allow limited elections. Oman's constitution declares the sharia to be the source of all legislation. In Kuwait, there have been stinging criticisms of moves towards secularisation.[27]

---

27 Dahlia Kholaif, 'Secularism calls slammed', *Arab Times*, n.d., available at:
   http://www.arabtimesonline.com/kuwaitnews/pagesdetails.asp?nid=16562&ccid=9

Even Turkey, which underwent a secularising revolution under Ataturk and after, is today under continuous pressure from Islamists to reintroduce sharia law; today, two-thirds of Turkish women wear the headscarf, something that would have been unthinkable in the early years of the Republic.[28] In 2008, a ban on wearing headscarves at university was lifted by the Turkish parliament.[29]

Genuine reform has been slow and limited. Attempts to change the law are often met by counter-attacks or devious ways of re-establishing the status quo. As Turkey moves towards EU membership, legislation is being tightened in many areas. There has been a crackdown on honour killings, with more men being prosecuted for carrying out these murders: in response, in order to save male killers, families are now insisting that 'dishonoured' girls commit suicide.[30]

---

28 Christina Lamb, 'Headscarf war threatens to split Turkey', *Sunday Times*, 6 May 2007, available at: http://www.timesonline.co.uk/tol/news/world/middle_east/article1752230.ece

29 'Turkey Lifts University Headscarf Ban', *Sky News*, 9 February 2008, available at: http://news.sky.com/skynews/article/0,,30200-1304785,00.html

30 Yael Lavie, 'Women Forced into "Honour Suicides"', *Sky News*, 13 November 2007, available at: http://news.sky.com/skynews/article/0,,30200-1292564,00.html

Even today, only two Muslim countries have abolished outright the law of polygamy, and there are efforts to have it made legally acceptable in the UK (see below). In Iran, temporary marriage (*muta* or 'pleasure' marriage) is encouraged by the regime.

'On the whole,' writes Eleanor Abdella Doumato, 'modern legislation regarding marriage and divorce has had limited effect in altering the inequalities between men and women in shariah family law.'[31]

What Does Sharia Law Cover?

Traditionally, sharia law encompasses the full range of human behaviour, from criminal matters (including activities that would not be considered crimes in the modern West, such as adultery, homosexuality, apostasy or wearing the wrong clothes in public); to worship (including prayer, fasting, and pilgrimage); to details of sexual relations between a husband and wife; to business affairs; to family law (such as marriage, divorce, custody of children, and inheritance); to dietary regulations (mainly in determining whether meat is halal or not, halal being a close approximation to the Jewish kosher; or in the prohibition of pork and alcohol); to clothing (particularly women's garb); to bodily matters (such as urination and defecation, depilation, the use of the toothbrush, purification after

---

31 Eleanor Abdella Doumato, 'Marriage and Divorce: modern practice', *Encyclopedia of Islam in the Modern World*, vol. 3, p. 52.

menstruation or sex); to international law (which is based on the law of jihad).

The many rulings and refinements on these matters make up a vast body of manuscript and published literature, with variations between the schools. Naturally, only a narrow range of laws and the rulings that govern them fall within the purview of sharia courts in the United Kingdom, though there have been cases of courts ruling on matters of criminal law.[32] It is also hard to determine whether rulings are passed on matters like apostasy, adultery, homosexuality, requests by Muslim women to marry non-Muslim men, conversion to other religions and so on. It is axiomatic that a court ruling that any of these 'crimes' is punishable (mainly by death) could influence individuals to take the law into their own hands, as already happens with 'honour' killings. Since the British state currently exercises no form of supervision over its sharia courts, we are left in the dark as to what is really going on.

Leyton's Islamic Sharia Law Council, like other sharia courts, deals in family law. Ninety-five per cent of its requests for arbitration have dealt with issues of divorce. This seems a high figure, since it leaves out marriage as such, financial and business matters, or

---

32 Murad Ahmed, Frances Gibb 'From Leyton to Dewsbury, sharia courts are already settling disputes', *The Times*, 8 February 2008, available at: http://www.timesonline.co.uk/tol/comment/faith/article3330 657.ece

judgements on matters like veiling, the alms-tax, sharia -compliant banking and mortgages, endowments, inheritance, and more—all of which are staples of the online fatwa sites that function as invisible sharia courts in the UK and internationally (see below).

Nevertheless, there can be no doubt that matters of personal and family law dominate the consultations that take place in British Muslim courts. Marriage and divorce are certainly central to this, but judgements made in this sector may touch on and can take us into sensitive and even illegal or semi-legal territory. Marriage in itself invites rulings on whether the bride may be underage or not; whether the husband may have sex with his wife even if she is underage; whether a husband may marry more than one wife; how much the dowry should be; and whether the bride's consent is needed in what is regarded as a civil contract between her male guardian (father, grandfather, uncle, etc.) and the groom.

Most recently, in May 2009, a British mother of Pakistani origin was jailed for three years on a charge of child sex offences and attempting to pervert the course of justice after she was found guilty of forcing her two daughters, one 14 and one 15, into marriages with cousins in Pakistan. Such marriages, where a girl is tricked into making a visit to relatives in Pakistan, are very common. In this case, a British court intervened after one of the daughters confided in a teacher. In Manchester Crown Court, Judge Clement Goldstone stated that:

Everyone is entitled to his or her beliefs and is to be encouraged to practise in accordance with those beliefs and to live a life which embraces the culture of those beliefs. But those who choose to live in this country and who, like you, are British subjects, must not abandon our laws in the practice of those beliefs and that culture. If they do, they will face the consequences.[33]

In 2004, ministers planned legislation which would make forcing someone to marry a criminal offence, but, following protests from the Muslim Association of Britain, these plans were dropped and have never become law. While the MCB treats every gesture aimed at improving the lives of British Muslims with contempt, and the government backs down every time they encounter Muslim protests, it is highly unlikely that any progress will be made.

Divorce raises further issues: does the woman have to return her dowry, does the husband have to pay maintenance, who has custody of the children (routinely the husband after the age of seven), what takes place if the couple want to re-marry (she has to marry and have intercourse with someone else first— see below), and so on? If a woman resorts to the court in order to divorce her husband, what grounds will be available to her, apart from the narrow range available in sharia law, the chief among these being impotence? In the case of a Shi'i court, will it permit temporary

---

33 http://www.dailymail.co.uk/news/article-1185589/Muslim-mother-forced-school-age-daughters-marry-cousins-jailed-3-years.html

marriage, which leaves the woman high and dry when the relationship comes to its end after a fixed period?

We have just referred to the situation in which a divorced couple wish to re-marry. The necessary legal device that allows them to do so is known as *halala*. Sharia law prescribes this 'solution' where a husband has divorced his wife (usually by three repeated statements of 'I divorce you') in a moment of thought-lessness or under pressure, regrets what he has done (even though it was done in private), and wishes to re-marry his wife. In this event, the wife must wait her *'idda*, three successive menstrual periods or, in Qur'anic terms, four months and ten days. This is to ensure she is not pregnant. On completion of the *'idda*, she must marry another man and have sexual intercourse with him. He must then divorce her. And she must observe a second *'idda*. Only then may she re-marry her original husband. Though considered legal, the process of *halala* is certain to prove traumatic for the wife, even though she was not the one to pronounce divorce in haste.

Attempts to reform sharia law in areas like this have met with opposition. On 8 August 2008, the Muslim Institute launched a model Muslim Marriage Contract[34] intending this to become a basis for the incorporation of Islamic marriage into UK civil law. It contained a number of refreshing modifications of the

---

34 See:
    http://www.muslimparliament.org.uk/Documentation/Muslim%20Marriage%20Contract.pdf

existing sharia code, freeing women of any need for a *wali* or guardian to act on their behalf and stipulating the automatic right of divorce to the wife, while allowing her to retain her financial rights. The model contract was endorsed by a number of heavyweight UK-based Islamic institutions, including the Muslim Council of Britain, the Imams and Mosques Council, the Muslim Law (Shariah) Council UK, the Utrujj Foundation, the Muslim Parliament of Great Britain, the City Circle, Muslim Women's Network-UK, the Fatima Network and the Muslim Community Helpline (Ex-MWH).

Despite this backing from such a wide range of Muslim bodies, the contract came under immediate and sustained criticism, notably from Shaykh Haytham al-Haddad of al-Muntada al-Islami and the Islamic Shariah Council. Haddad (and the ISC) lambasted the MCB and others for creating what they termed an 'anti-Islamic' document. Haddad delivered a long address[35] in condemnation of the contract. His comments make interesting listening for the extent to which they predict a hard time ahead for anyone wanting to bring sharia into the UK legal system.

Haddad begins by asserting that Islam is perfect, and that it is suitable for all times and places, and it is unbelief (*kufr*) to deny this. (This is a standard position for all Muslim clerics: to say that Islam is imperfect

---

35 See YouTube video
http://uk.youtube.com/watch?v=FGRA252Y9BU and
following videos

would be a serious act of apostasy.) Innovation (*bid'a*) is forbidden. Some Muslims want to reform Islam to suit the West, a desire with which he strongly disagrees. He goes on to point out that the Muslim Institute contract stipulates that witnesses need not be Muslims, but people of good character from any religion. This he condemns. Again, the contract does not say witnesses should be two men, but could allow two women. This he condemns. The contract permits a woman to be married without a male guardian (*wali*) to act on her behalf. This he condemns. The contract gives a wife permission to divorce, but al-Haddad says only men have that right. (In Islamic law, a wife seeking a divorce must receive her husband's permission to do so.)

The arguments against the contract continue for some time, but it should be clear from the foregoing that a severe problem exists for any attempt to improve a system of legislation. This is made sharper by the MCB's own response to these criticisms, in which they back away from any suggestion that the document they backed (and, presumably, read) could be interpreted as a modern or reformist view of the sharia:[36]

MCB's STATEMENT: Muslim Marriage Certificate
August 18, 2008.

---

36 http://maqasid.wordpress.com/2008/08/18/mcbs-statement-muslim-marriage-certificate/

MCB clarifies its position on document initiated by the Muslim Institute.

In furtherance of its policy to work with others for the unity of Muslims and for the common good, the MCB had collaborated on a worthwhile initiative on enabling parties to a Muslim marriage to understand and respect their rights and obligations and to enable Courts to enforce the rights of parties in accordance with what is agreed at the time of the Nikah. That initiative has regrettably led to misinterpretation of Shari'ah by those who the MCB had trusted to take the lead on this matter. Those representing the Muslim Institute were reported as saying that the documentation produced was a 're-invention of Shari'ah' or that it was a 'modern' or 'reformist' view of the Shari'ah. These types of glib generalisations on sharia councils are unhelpful and not in keeping with MCB's evidence-based approach to community issues. Moreover the MCB looks to the traditional Islamic institutions of ijma (the consensus of scholars) as the way forward in resolving the issues of our times.

The MCB rejects the misguided and incorrect assertions made by and ascribed to the Muslim Institute.

'In the circumstances the MCB has decided to produce its own guidance which it will issue after due consultation with its affiliates and ulema' said Dr Reefat Drabu, Assistant Secretary General and the Chair of the Social & Family Affairs Committee of the MCB.

It is obvious that a great many of the issues that are raised in sharia courts have a direct bearing on the rights of women. Since many women from Britain's Pakistani, Bangladeshi, Indian, Somali and other Muslim communities may not be in the courts by free consent, there is a likelihood that some form of coercion exists to deprive them of rights that are due to them under British and European legislation. The incidence of honour killings within some Muslim communities suggests an atmosphere in which it is nearly impossible for women and girls to access or assert those rights without suffering penalties. Demands in much Islamic literature from Saudi and related sources, including fatwa sites, that women must remain inside their homes and may only go out, if at all, with their husband's consent and when fully veiled, raise the question of whether such considerations play a part in sharia court rulings.

The question of women's rights set against sharia provisions was brought starkly into the public arena in October of 2008, when the House of Lords decreed that sharia was incompatible with human rights. The ruling came in regard to the case of a Lebanese woman who sought asylum in the UK in order to avoid being sent back to Lebanon with her 12-year-old son. In Lebanon, the sharia law of custody would have forced her to hand the boy over to her violently abusive husband, on the grounds that a male child belongs to his father after the age of seven, regardless of other circumstances. 'The Lords stated that these provisions breached the mother's rights to family life and the right against discrimination and were severely disruptive to the child.'[37] In ruling in favour of the mother, Lord Hope

---

37 Afua Hirsch, 'Sharia law incompatible with human rights legislation, Lords say', *Guardian*, 23 October 2008, at: http://www.guardian.co.uk/world/2008/oct/23/religion-islam.

stated that: 'The place of the mother in the life of a child under that system is quite different under that law from that which is guaranteed [by the European Convention on Human Rights] ... it is discriminatory, too, because it denies women custody of their children after they have reached the age of custodial transfer simply because they are women.'[38] Lord Hope also introduced a wider dimension than British law: the European Convention on Human Rights. The legal director of Liberty, which took the woman's case to the Lords, asked: 'How can the government speak of equal treatment in one breath and seek to deport mother and child to face separation under sharia law in another? The Law Lords have rightly upheld basic protections which must be available to us all.'[39]

Several bodies, including the Association of Muslim Lawyers and the Muslim Council of Britain, have been trying to negotiate an acceptance of sharia law within this country. Hajj Ahmad Thomson of the AML has been to the forefront in arguing the Muslim case. His principal concern is not human rights in general, but how human rights legislation may be used to secure

---

38 Quoted in Afua Hirsch, 'Sharia law incompatible with human rights legislation, Lords say', *Guardian*, 23 October 2008.

39 'Mother facing separation from her son under Shari'a law granted refuge by Law Lords', *Liberty*, 22 October 2008, at: http://www.liberty-human-rights.org.uk/news-and-events/1-press-releases/2008/22-10-08-mother-facing-separation-from-her-son-granted-refuge.shtml.

Muslim rights, such as the right to incorporate what he calls 'Muslim Personal Law' into UK domestic law. '...[T]he government,' he writes, 'remains by virtue of *Articles 1, 13 and 14* of the *ECHR* (European Convention on Human Rights) under an international legal duty to secure these rights by providing a remedy if a Muslim's religious rights are violated.'[40] He then says: 'It is arguable that this international legal duty also includes the duty to secure these rights by incorporating Muslim personal law into UK domestic law, including the legal recognition of Muslim marriages, divorces and inheritance.'[41]

Leaving expert legal comment to one side, it should be clear that Thomson's argument is a form of special pleading that creates more problems than it purports to solve. If the incorporation of Islamic law is acceptable, why should Chinese-origin citizens not ask for the introduction of Chinese personal law, or Indian-origin citizens for Indian personal law? The reason, of course, is that they have become citizens of the UK and have, through the conferral of citizenship, opted to be ruled by UK law. If I were to take up residence in Iran and

---

40 Hajj Ahmad Thomson, 'Incorporating Muslim Personal Law into UK Domestic Law', *AMSS* (Association of Muslim Social Scientists) *UK 5th Annual Conference — Fiqh Today*, 22 February 2004, p. 1, at: http://www.wynnechambers.co.uk/pdf/AMSS-ATNotes220204.pdf

41 Thomson, 'Incorporating Muslim Personal Law into UK Domestic Law', 2004.

take citizenship, then I would have to abandon my right to British liberties and agree to live under a more restrictive code. There is no reason why religion should trump citizenship in the legal area.

Thomson himself illustrates the patent absurdity of tracking his own argument to its logical conclusion. 'Clearly the same arguments apply to other minority faith-based communities, such as, for example the Jews, the Hindus and the Sikhs... If everyone in our present multi-ethnic, multi-cultural, multi-faith society is to be treated equally by the law, then recognition of the various religious communities' personal law is necessary in achieving a balance between equality and diversity.'[42]

If 'personal law' referred only to rules dictating diet, acts of worship, and dress, this would happen naturally and without any need for recourse to legal statutes. But the areas in which Thomson and other Muslim proponents of incorporation would introduce sharia have much more than a purely personal connotation. As Thomson himself puts it, problems may arise 'as regards the duties and rights between spouses and divorcees, the legal status of their children, ownership of property, eligibility to state benefits and dealing with public authorities in general,

---

42 Thomson, 'Incorporating Muslim Personal Law into UK Domestic Law', 2004.

especially when travelling abroad and when death occurs.'[43]

He takes it further than this, however: 'At present witnesses in the secular courts are permitted to hold their holy book in their right hand when swearing to tell the truth, but lawyers cannot base their legal argument on what the holy books say—and judges cannot give judgement in accordance with the criteria or commands and prohibitions which these holy books contain.'

To take this literally (which seems to be the intention) would mean that a source of law deemed infallible and above all secular legal systems would be enforced in Britain. That would entail debate over how these books would be interpreted, or by which school of law. However, Thomson argues that secular courts would not be the proper places for religious argument and judgement, but 'appropriately constituted religious courts'. Given that, as we have seen and will see, sharia is frequently contradictory to Western law codes and the principles on which they are based and has in one instance thus far been deemed 'incompatible with human rights', it is hard to see how a parallel legal system, however restricted, would be of benefit to British citizens, including Muslims who did not want to be ruled by Islamic law.

---

43 Thomson, 'Incorporating Muslim Personal Law into UK Domestic Law', 2004.

The inappropriateness of a separate jurisdiction comes across clearly in Thomson's arguments about the implementation of sharia in the UK:

(i)   Provided that this matter is approached and dealt with in the right way, it is feasible for legislation to be enacted so that:

(ii)   Muslim marriages (including polygamous marriages up to the maximum of four wives as permitted by the sharia of Allah) and divorces are recognised as legally valid by the law of the land.

(iii)   Since the Sharia of Islam permits a Muslim man to marry up to four wives provided that he maintains them and their children as equally as is possible, the law of bigamy is amended so as to make allowance for valid Muslim marriages.

If marrying more than one woman were of no greater moment than another man's cohabiting with two or more women, bigamy would not need to be criminalised. But legal marriage entails numerous legal benefits and restraints and carries implications for children, inheritance and property. And since Islamic law — regardless of what its apologists argue — discriminates against women in and out of the married state, it can never be in conformity with British legislation. If Muslim women here are British citizens, then they are entitled to exactly the same freedoms and protections as other British women.

In practice, this is difficult to achieve. One of the greatest problems Muslim women in this country (and elsewhere) face is obtaining divorces from unco-operative husbands (in parallel with the difficulty they experience in being too easily divorced by the three talaq formula). This, in turn, may lead to more serious problems for the woman. According to James Brandon and Salam Hafez, authors of a study of honour-based violence in the UK: 'Muslim women are often unable to escape domestic violence or abusive partners because imams are unwilling to allow them to initiate divorces.'[44]

Islamic marriages are given priority over civil ones, meaning that women may not have recourse to civil courts should they wish to break free from an abusive husband. Brandon and Hafez write that:

> Without an Islamic wedding, communities will regard a couple as 'living in sin'—even if they have had a UK civil marriage—which can lead to them being ostracised from the community or face violence. Rehana Bibi, a domestic violence advisor at Hyndburn and Ribble Valley Outreach in Accrington, says: 'If you're Asian, the community doesn't see it as necessary to have English marriages—but you have to have an Islamic marriage.' But while numerous laws have made it easier for women to obtain civil divorces on the grounds of domestic violence or sexual abuse, this is not always true for Islamic marriages.

---

44 Brandon, J. and Hafez, S., *Crimes of the Community: Honour-based Violence in the UK*, London: Centre for Social Cohesion, 2008, p. 98.

Although Islamic law does not permit or counsel honour killings, these continue to take place within the Muslim community. It is hard not to see some connection between these extra-judicial killings and the attitude of sharia to the infringement of sexual mores. Extra-marital sex is punished in some Islamic states by the *hudud* punishments of flogging and execution, and this severity may play a role in convincing some Muslims that such transgressions are crimes rather than peccadilloes (or less), that the law of beheading or stoning indicates the seriousness of these 'crimes', and that families may only regain their honour by dispatching a straying daughter or sister. Some of the online fatwa sites carry statements to the effect that properly-instituted sharia law compels the flogging of unmarried individuals and the execution (usually by stoning, a most hideous and cruel punishment) of married adulterers. The same rulings usually indicate that these punishments should not be carried out in a non-Muslim state, but it may be argued that when this notion of a divine punishment is fused with communal pressures it may, in come cases, lead to barbarous treatment, ranging from incarceration to murder. How this can be resolved, given that Islamic law is deemed immutable, is a very serious problem for our society and even more serious for Muslim societies struggling to make a meaningful transition to modernity.

Thomson moves beyond personal law when he argues for a significant change in the British financial system, again based on sharia provisions. '... [T]he practice of usury... should be made illegal once more—

or at least unenforceable in a court of law.' The problems with this are numerous, but they may be summed up in one simple statement: if sharia law permitted interest, Thomson would be arguing in favour of it. Modern secular legal systems are built on rationality, not on arbitrary pronouncements of presumed divine or traditional origin.

But there is another issue here. This is gradualism, the doctrine that Islamic law must be introduced into Western systems in a piecemeal fashion. Dr Yusuf al-Qaradawi, who is head of the European Council for Fatwa and Research, has argued that:

> Gradualism is to be observed when it comes to applying the rulings of the Shari'ah in today's life when Muslims have been socially, legislatively, and culturally invaded... Gradualism here refers to preparing people ideologically, psychologically, morally, and socially to accept and adopt the application of the Shari'ah in all aspects of life, and to finding lawful alternatives for the forbidden principles upon which many associations have been founded for so long.

> Gradualism in that sense does not mean we are to procrastinate and put off applying the Shari'ah. Gradualism is not to be taken as a pretext for discouraging people and foiling their pressing demands to establish Allah's laws.[45]

---

45 Yusuf al-Qaradawi, 'Gradualism in Applying the Shari'ah', *Islam Online*, 26 April 2005, at:
    http://www.islamonline.net/servlet/Satellite?c=Article_C&ci
    d=1209357806230&pagename=Zone-English-
    Living_Shariah%2FLSELayout.

If we understand this correctly, al-Qaradawi, who holds a mixture of moderate and extreme views, envisages a gradual process through which sharia legislation is applied 'in all aspects of life', something that would, presumably, take us well beyond matters of personal law. The implication is that, if sharia can be established in principle within a non-Muslim legal system, it will only be a matter of time before the range of its application is extended beyond whatever was originally intended.

In 2005, the well-known Islamic intellectual Tariq Ramadan, a man noted for the balancing act he performs between public moderation and private radicalism,[46] made a call for an international moratorium on the application of the *hudud* punishments (such as execution for adultery or the cutting off of hands for theft). In his statement, Ramadan cites the injustice of these punishments as a crucial reason for imposing a moratorium: 'A still more grave injustice is that these penalties are applied almost exclusively to women and the poor, the doubly victimised, never to the wealthy, the powerful, or the oppressors.'[47]

---

46 For an analysis of Ramadan's mixed messages, see Fourest, C., *Brother Tariq: The Doublespeak of Tariq Ramadan*, London, 2008.

47 News Staff, 'Tariq Ramadan Calls for Hudud Freeze', *Islam Online*, 30 March 2005, at: http://www.islamonline.net/servlet/Satellite?c=Article_C&cid=1209357916175&pagename=Zone-English-Living_Shariah%2FLSELayout. For the full text of

He continues: 'Furthermore, hundreds of prisoners have no access to anything that could even remotely be called defense counsel. Death sentences are decided and carried out against women, men and even minors (political prisoners, traffickers, delinquents, etc.) without ever given [sic] a chance to obtain legal counsel.'

Whatever Ramadan's own motives in calling for this freeze, its reception by Muslim clerics was both inevitable and disturbing. Almost without exception, they rounded on him and the moratorium as an attempt to undermine Islam. Given Ramadan's extremely high reputation in the Islamic world, especially in Europe, and his status as the grandson of Hasan al-Banna' the founder of the Muslim Brotherhood, this refusal to listen to his recommendation illustrates how very difficult it has become to advocate even temporary reform, even in an area where a modern consciousness would at once recognize a serious obstacle to Muslim progress. An illogical linkage is made between Ramadan's call for a cessation of clearly barbaric punishments and a supposed threat to all forms of sharia law, and even the sharia in its entirety. 'If we call today for an international moratorium on corporal punishment, stoning and the death penalty, then tomorrow I am so worried that

Ramadan's call, see 'An International call for Moratorium on corporal punishment, stoning and the death penalty in the Islamic world', at:
http://www.tariqramadan.com/spip.php?article264.

they may ask Muslims to suspend their Friday Prayer,' said Sano Koutoub Moustapha, a member of the Islamic Fiqh [Jurisprudence] Academy attached to the Organization of the Islamic Conference, the leading international organisation of Muslim states.[48]

A similar response came from Muzammil H. Siddiqi, President of the Fiqh Council of North America and former President of the Islamic Society of North America: 'Some may start calling for a moratorium on the family law of Islam also, and some others on the business and finance laws of Islam, and some may ask for [a] moratorium on the whole *Shari'ah*'.

Although the proposed moratorium is not relevant to the UK, where corporal punishments do not take place, the widespread response to it, even from Muslim authorities living in the West, is an important indicator of the extent to which Islamic clerics insist on the absolute integrity of the system. To remove one part of the sharia invites its total dissolution. This is similar to (and linked to) the view that, to alter even one letter of the Qur'an or the Hadith literature invites a more wholesale challenge to the texts and the authority they exercise.

If the more egregious aspects of the sharia such as stoning may not be laid aside, even temporarily, how much harder it will prove to dismantle the divorce

---

48 News Staff, 'Tariq Ramadan Calls for Hudud Freeze', *Islam Online*, 30 March 2005.

laws or those relating to wider restrictions on the independence of women.

And, even if the laws for the punishment of homosexuals or apostates may not be applied in the UK, the many rulings that treat execution as valid in such cases can only reinforce deep-seated prejudices and hatred. To the extent that Muslims are taught to consider homosexuality as a crime or apostasy as grievous sin encouraged by the principle of free choice in religion, sanctioned by human rights law, Muslim individuals and families will find it harder than it need be to live in Western society without finding them-selves in daily conflict with some of the noblest values Western civilisation has brought into being. For our social and legal systems to indulge prejudices like these while we continue to fight racism, homophobia and even Islamophobia throughout the rest of society is one indulgence too many. If Muslim schools do not teach their pupils that gay men and women are human beings with rights, or that changing one's religion is a basic human right, or that women have exactly the same rights as men, then we have to find other ways in which these important lessons may be taught and learned. If we could educate a new generation of Muslims to understand issues like human rights better, there might be some hope that they would demand changes in *sharia* law, and perhaps its suspension except in matters of worship and ethics, which are hardly contentious.

Traditionally, sharia has been applied with the assumption that Muslims are in the majority and rule the country. For centuries, this is how things normally stood: there were relatively few Muslims who lived in non-Muslim states. This meant that little need was seen to modify sharia rulings in order to suit the non-Muslim environment, not least because there were no mechanisms in place to enforce even personal law.

This situation changed dramatically from the early nineteenth century onwards, first in situations where Muslims found themselves ruled by the European imperial powers, then as Muslims entered countries in which they represented small, but growing and permanent minorities. Across Europe, Muslim numbers have moved into the millions,[49] and this has prompted many clerics to look more closely at ways in which sharia may be applied in situations where it does not constitute the law of the land.

Foremost among those who have sought to tackle the many dilemmas sharia poses in non-Muslim societies are the Iraqi Shaykh Taha Jabir al-'Alwani (1935-) and the better known Egyptian Shaykh Yusuf al-Qaradawi (1926-). Al-'Alwani emigrated to the United States in 1983, where he founded the Fiqh Council of North America, the leading American organisation for Islamic law. He has been a founder-

---

49 These figures break down roughly as follows: Albania 2.2m; Austria 339,000; Belgium 0.4m; Bosnia 1.5m; Denmark 270,000; France 6m; Germany 3m; Italy 825,000; Macedonia 630,000; The Netherlands 1m; Serbia 1.8m; Spain 1m; Sweden 300,000; Switzerland 311,000; UK 2m. The European total reaches to around 21,500,000.

member of the Council of the Muslim World League, a key organisation in Saudi/Wahhabi missionary work; and a member of the Organization of the Islamic Conference Fiqh Academy in Jeddah, Saudi Arabia. In 1997, he joined with al-Qaradawi in founding the European Council for Fatwa and Research. The FCNA, the ECFR, and the Islamic Fiqh Academy in India are all connected to the OIC through the Jeddah Fiqh Academy. Taken together, they exercise a powerful influence on Muslims seeking sharia solutions to modern problem.

Al-'Alwani coined a useful new term to describe jurisprudential work for Muslims in non-Muslim countries: *Fiqh al-Aqalliyyat*, the Jurisprudence of Minorities. This has since become the standard form for legal discussion of this kind, but it would be a mistake to think it is always reformist in a positive sense. According to Shammai Fishman, '*Fiqh al-aqalliyyat* is squarely in the utilitarian camp and the tradition of the *salafiyya* movement.'[50] Salafism, which started in Egypt in the early years of the twentieth century, has a close affinity with Wahhabism in its insistence that only the Qur'an, the Prophetic Traditions and the views of the first three generations

---

50 Shammai Fishman, *Fiqh al-Aqalliyyat: A Legal Theory for Muslim Minorities*, Center on Islam, Democracy, and the Future of the Muslim World, Hudson Institute, Washington, 2006, at:
http://www.futureofmuslimworld.com/docLib/20061018_MonographFishman2.pdf

of Muslims may be used to form legal and doctrinal opinions. It is backward-looking and restrictive. This approach is exemplified by al-'Alwani's insistence on the Islamisation of knowledge. Rather than Muslims directly borrowing Western scientific achievement, the intention is to use the Qur'an and other Islamic sources to turn science into something more acceptable to religious doctrine.

Al-Qaradawi, who is based in Qatar, is a popular broadcaster and a leading figure in the Muslim Brotherhood. He runs an important and popular website, IslamOnline, where fatwas on a wide range of issues are provided and articles on political issues of the day published.

Al-Qaradawi's views on minority fiqh are set out in a work entitled *Fi fiqh al-aqalliyyat al-muslima: hayat al-muslimin wast al-mujtama'at al-ukhra*, translated as *Fiqh of Muslim Minorities: Contentious issues and recommended solutions*.[51] It is clear from the beginning that al-Qaradawi is unwilling to bend very much to adapt Islamic law to Western situations. Muslims are bound, he says, by all of the sharia, regardless of where they may be.[52] Not only that, but the Qur'an and Sunna are to be accepted 'as a whole not partially'.[53] Compromise is clearly not part of this formula.

---

51 *Fiqh of Muslim Minorities*, English translation published by al-Falah Foundation, Cairo, 2003.

52 *Fiqh of Muslim Minorities*, pp. xiii-xiv.

53 *Fiqh of Muslim Minorities*, p. xv.

In similar vein, al-Qaradawi opposes any attempt to bring religions together through interfaith initiatives, but is happy for Muslims to seek to convert non-Muslims. He will accept cooperation between faiths in order to cooperate against atheism or vice.[54]

In a number of fatwas reprinted in this text, he puts forward several positions that retain a deeply traditionalist and intolerant view of things. A Muslim woman may not marry a Muslim Communist.[55] If a Muslim woman leaves Islam after marriage, the marriage must be dissolved.[56] The punishment for apostasy is killing or imprisonment.[57] A Muslim may not marry a Baha'i woman.[58] Muslims may not marry Jewish women so long as the struggle between Israel and Muslims continues. 'Each Jewish woman is in spirit a soldier in the army of Israel.'[59] Here, as elsewhere, where al-Qaradawi breaks with tradition (Muslim men are permitted to marry Jewish women), he does so in a spirit of less, not greater tolerance. Muslim men are not allowed to marry non-Muslim women in general if this means Muslim women can't find husbands (since they

54 *Fiqh of Muslim Minorities*, pp. 15ff.

55 *Fiqh of Muslim Minorities*, p. 55.

56 *Fiqh of Muslim Minorities*, p. 62.

57 *Fiqh of Muslim Minorities*, p. 63.

58 *Fiqh of Muslim Minorities*, p. 63.

59 *Fiqh of Muslim Minorities*, p. 71.

are only permitted to marry Muslim men).[60] 'Marrying non-Muslim women in our age should be prohibited… It should be made permissible only in cases of dire necessity.'[61]

In a lengthy section, he presents a variety of juridical opinions as to whether a female convert to Islam is obliged to separate from (and divorce) her non-Muslim husband. (This also applies to a male convert and his non-Muslim wife.) He concludes that Muslims and unbelievers cannot marry.[62]

Finally, he disagrees with the majority opinion, which holds that a Muslim cannot inherit from a non-Muslim. But the opposite cannot hold: 'Dhimmis [Jews and Christians] do not inherit from Muslims'.[63]

Given that al-Qaradawi is one of the most influential Muslim scholars alive today, the general tenor of these and similar rulings found on his IslamOnline website (see below) bodes ill for the use of *Fiqh al-Aqalliyyat* as a medium for furthering tolerance, understanding and social cohesion for Muslims living in the West. If anything, the fatwas issued from this perspective are retrogressive rather than modernising.

Possibly more worrying is the role played in this by scholars and councils based in Muslim states (as in the

---

60 *Fiqh of Muslim Minorities*, pp. 72-73.

61 *Fiqh of Muslim Minorities*, p. 78.

62 *Fiqh of Muslim Minorities*, pp. 79-116.

63 *Fiqh of Muslim Minorities*, pp. 117ff.

influence of al-Qaradawi, who is based in Qatar, as exercised through the European Council for Fatwa and Research or through IslamOnline). Extra-territorial legal opinions and judgement can enter countries like the UK by the back door and may have serious consequences here.

Shammai Fishman cites a particularly worrying example of this, linked to al-Alwani and al-Qaradawi:

> Al-Alwani is also deeply involved in matters concerning Muslims who serve in the United States Armed Forces. During the first month after the September 11 terrorist attacks, al-Alwani received a question from Capt. Abd al-Rashid Muhammad, a Muslim military chaplain stationed in Walter Reed Army Medical Center in Washington, asking if Muslim soldiers could fight in Afghanistan. An account of the events exists in a MEMRI report.[64]

Al-Alwani's mild actions are worthy of being studied in light of his doctrine. The first thing Al-Alwani did was to forward the question to a special committee headed by Shaykh Dr Yousef al-Qaradawi. Al-Qaradawi's committee gave a ruling allowing the Muslim soldiers 'to be united against all those who terrorize the innocent', and on this basis al-Alwani issued a similar ruling for the Muslim troops. The twist in the story

---

64 MEMRI report in English (No. 75, 6 November 2001). See on-line in:
    http://www.memri.de/uebersetzungen_analysen/themen/usa
    _und_der_nahe_osten/us_american_muslim_06_11_01.html

happened two weeks later, when in a Friday sermon al-Qaradawi denounced his first ruling.[65]

What did al-Alwani gain for the Muslim minorities by this controversial move? The answer lies in the question. Almost without noticing, al-Alwani created a factual situation wherein the orders of Muslim soldiers in the US Army are open to question and negotiation. The idea that Muslims who serve in the US army should do it with the consent of foreign Muslim scholars, and according to their conditions, was put on the table. Al-Alwani, through his actions, introduced the reality that the United States Federal Government should no longer automatically take the loyalty of Muslims to the US Army for granted. This should be considered as a great victory for the doctrine of Muslim Minority Jurisprudence, especially since it was achieved without backfire from the Western media.[66]

Similar issues have been raised about Muslims serving in the British army or police force.

A member of a chatroom run by the Followers of Ahl us-Sunnah wal-Jamaa'ah said joining the British Army or police is 'clearly haram [forbidden] and a sin.' One leading member of the group said that anyone

---

65 www.asharqalawsat.com 14 October 2001.

66 Shammai Fishman, 'Some Notes on Arabic Terminology as a Link Between Tariq Ramadan and Shaykh Dr Taha Jabir al-Alwani, Founder of the Doctrine of "Muslim Minority Jurisprudence" (*Fiqh al-Aqaliyyat al-Muslimah*)', The Project for the Research of Islamist Movements (PRISM), Herzliya, Israel, n.d.

who did the following was a non-believer: 'applying for jobs that are asking Muslims to join the MI5 to infiltrate the community; co-operating with the Government by asking Muslim parents to spy on their children; working with deviant sects who ask us to join the crusading British Army; swearing an oath of allegiance to the fallible Queen'.[67]

Perhaps the most worrying way in which external judgements may find force within the UK legal system would be in cases involving acts of religious discrimination or, were there to be a future extended law of blasphemy, in cases alleging blasphemous intent by authors, cartoonists or broadcasters. Even where Islamic rulings from British clerics were advanced as 'evidence' that a certain book was blasphemous or a specific action discriminatory, it is highly likely that the clerics would have had recourse to external authorities of greater distinction than themselves, to the European Centre for Fatwas and Research or even to al-Azhar University. A British judge or jury could not rule against a Muslim authority (who would be deemed best placed to know what constituted blasphemy or discrimination against Muslims), which would mean that a British court would always be at the mercy of

---

67 Duncan Gardham, 'Websites denounce British Muslim Soldiers', *The Telegraph*, 2 February 2007, at: http://www.telegraph.co.uk/news/uknews/1541390/Websites -denounce-British-Muslim-soldiers.html. See this same article for other examples.

external rulings. In the end, that would expose UK law and UK courts to inappropriate pressure.

In January 2007, Aziz Shaykh, a professor in the Division of Community Health Services at Edinburgh University, published an article in the *British Medical Journal*[68] in which he argued that Muslims must have entirely separate health services from the rest of the community. A debate emerged from this that may be read online. The danger Shaykh's argument presents is that Muslims will become the only group to receive preferential treatment on purely religious grounds. Since many Muslim authorities argue against the mixing of Muslims and non-Muslims, and since they base this discriminatory position on sharia law, this would open up yet another portal through which external religio-legal pressure would be brought to bear in Britain. To the extent that *Fiqh al-Aqalliyyat* is developed outside the UK by thinkers like al-Alwani, al-Qaradawi or Tariq Ramadan, demands will continue to be made for preferential treatment for Muslims in all areas of life. Rather than a way forward towards enhanced social cohesion and wider integration, it may become a barrier to Muslims for achieving genuine

---

68 Aziz Shaykh, 'Should Muslims have faith-based health services?', *BMJ*, 13 January 2007, at: http://www.bmj.com/cgi/content/full/334/7584/74.

autonomy within the context of Western values and freedoms.[69]

Despite the ubiquity of fatwas online and the growing body of pronouncements made by the practitioners of *Fiqh al-Aqalliyyat*, an indeterminate number of sharia courts or tribunals have emerged and are currently working in the UK. Their decisions are legally binding and can be enforced by county courts and high courts provided both parties in a case have agreed to be ruled by sharia law. Most reports cite five courts as working in this way, based in London, Birmingham, Bradford, Coventry, and Manchester. However, our investigations indicate that a considerably larger number—85 at least—are operating, mainly out of mosques dotted around the country. There are, to begin with, 13 tribunals operating within a network administered by the Islamic Sharia Council (ISC) based in Leyton. (This network also has two tribunals working abroad.) Second, there are three non-ISC courts run by the Association of Muslim Lawyers (AML). Thirdly, there are three further councils belonging neither to the ISC nor the AML. Finally, there are the dozens of informal tribunals run out of mosques or online (like the Darul Iftaa in Leicester). A few mosques also offer an online fatwa service or links to online fatwa sites. Some

---

[69] For more on the modern application of sharia, see Abbas Amanat and Frank Griffel (eds), *Shari'a: Islamic Law in the Contemporary Context*, Stanford University Press, 2007.

of these sites are also accessible from a number of Muslim schools.

That many of these tribunals function in an unofficial capacity and do not liaise with the civil authorities arouses concern as to the legality of their rulings. Since it is extremely difficult to gain access to these tribunals, we have tried to show what sort of rulings they may give by referring to online sites used by mosques and individuals. It will at once be clear that the muftis who issue these fatwas walk a very fine line between legality and illegality and sometimes cross into territory where human rights are abused. It should be borne in mind that sharia rulings do not fluctuate by very much (though variants between muftis are far from uncommon). This principle, that it is obligatory to uphold the essential integrity of Islamic jurisprudence and the rulings that come from it, allows us to show in broad terms what muftis are ruling by referring to online sites that are referenced by some of the mosques in our list. The Appendix below provides a range of rulings gleaned from some of these sites, where archives are kept of past fatwas, together with the questions that prompted them. We have edited this material lightly in order to make it accessible to the non-Muslim and non-specialist.

Among the rulings in the Appendix, we find some that advise illegal actions and others that transgress human rights standards as they are applied by British court. Here are some examples: a Muslim woman may not under any circumstances marry a non-Muslim man unless he converts to Islam; such a woman's children will be separated from her until she marries a Muslim man; polygamous marriage (i.e. two to four wives) is considered legal; a man may divorce his wife without telling her about it, provided he does not seek to sleep with her; a husband has conjugal rights over his wife, and she should normally answer his summons to have sex (but she cannot summon him for the same reason); a woman may not stay with her husband if he leaves Islam; non-Muslims may be deprived of their share in an inheritance; a divorce does not require witnesses (i.e. a man may divorce his wife and send her away even if no-one else knows about it); re-marriage requires the wife to marry, have sex with, and be divorced by another man; a wife has no property rights in the event of divorce (which may be initiated arbitrarily by her husband); sharia law must override the judgements of British courts; rights of child custody may differ from those in UK law; taking up residence in a non-Muslim country except for limited reasons is forbidden; taking out insurance is prohibited, even if required by law; there is no requirement to register a marriage according to the law of the country; polygamy is acceptable, even if against the law; it is undesirable to rent an apartment belonging to a Christian church; a Muslim lawyer has to act contrary to UK law where it contradicts sharia; employment through driving a taxi is prohibited; it is allowable to be a police officer, provided one is not called upon to do anything contrary to sharia; women are restricted in leaving their homes and driving cars; an adult woman may not marry anyone she chooses; sharia law of legitimacy contradicts the Legitimacy Act 1976; a woman may not leave her home without her husband's consent (which may constitute false imprisonment); legal adoption is forbidden; a man may coerce his wife to have sex; a woman may not retain custody of her child after seven (for a boy) or nine (for a girl); a civil marriage may be considered invalid; sharia law takes priority over secular law (e.g. a wife may not divorce her husband in a civil court); fighting the Americans and British is a religious duty; recommendation of severe punishments for homosexuals; a woman's recourse to fertility treatment is disliked; a woman cannot marry without the presence (and permission) of a male guardian (the *wali*); a divorce is valid if the husband simply intends to do it; polygamous marriage should be maintained, even in the UK; if a woman's *'idda* has expired and she no longer has marital relations with her husband, he is excused alimony payments; an illegitimate child may not inherit from his/her father.

Most of these are in little need of comment, but they often have to be read in their full form to see the kind of arguments that are used to justify them. If put into practice, they would undermine UK law by allowing a single community to play fast and loose with British law and customs. They are divisive, many of them are discriminatory against women and non-Muslims, and they deeply undermine the freedoms that all British citizens are entitled to enjoy. A woman should not be denied fertility treatment just because she is a Muslim, nor should a man be permitted to contract polygamous marriages with impunity. The introduction of sharia law into this country is a recipe for a dichotomous legal system that holds Muslims and non-Muslims to different standards. This is not a matter of eating halal meat or seeking God's blessing on one's marriage. It is a challenge to what we believe to be the rights and freedoms of the individual, to our concept of a legal system based on what parliament enacts, and to the right of all of us to live in a society as free as possible from ethnic-religious division or communal claims to superiority and a special status that puts them in some respects above the law to which we are all bound.

Appendix

Summary of Online Fatwas

Fatwas online

1. Sunnipath (Woking Mosque link)

A Muslim woman may marry a non-Muslim man

<u>Sunnipath</u>
<u>http://qa.sunnipath.com/issue_view.asp?HD=7&ID=15</u>
<u>113&CATE=1436</u>

Question ID: 15113; Date Published: August 01, 2007
Answered by Ustadha Zaynab Ansari, SunniPath
Academy Teacher

Question:
The questioner's friend has an older sister who was
married to a difficult man. The sister obtained a
divorce, and now she has decided to marry a non-
Muslim. This man is good to her and is morally
upright. How should the friend handle this, knowing
that the sister's decision is not acceptable religiously?

Answer:
The respondent indicates that marrying a non-Muslim
man remains 'impermissible', despite the sister's bad
experiences with Muslim men. She is sinning and must
be told that her wish to marry this man is 'unlawful'.
The only acceptable solution is for the non-Muslim
fiancé to convert. The friend must not allow her
children to stay in the sister's home until this is done.

Acceptance of polygamous marriage

Sunnipath

http://qa.sunnipath.com/issue_view.asp?HD=3&ID=69
69&CATE=250

Answered by Ustadha Zaynab Ansari, SunniPath
Academy Teacher

Question:
The questioner is her husband's second wife, but their
marriage is a secret, even from their families. They
have been married three years. She is much neglected
by her husband, who sees her for an hour every six to
eight weeks, and who won't even speak to her by
telephone.

Answer:
The respondent agrees that this is a difficult situation
and even advises the questioner to consider ending the
marriage. But at no point does she find fault with the
root problem, namely the polygamous nature of the
marriage. That is taken for granted as acceptable. 'Your
husband has been dishonest to both of his wives. You
have a right to be recognized as your husband's wife.
Secret marriages are not permitted in Islam.'

A man may keep divorce secret from his wife

Sunnipath

http://qa.sunnipath.com/issue_view.asp?HD=3&ID=77
51&CATE=251

Answered by Shaykh Amjad Rasheed

Question:

The questioner challenges an earlier ruling that said a man may divorce his wife without telling her he has done so, and cites situations in which this could lead to serious problems.

Answer:

The original ruling is defended on the grounds that such is the consensus of Islamic scholars and that 'the husband can independently effect divorce because divorce is not a contract [between two parties], but rather it is a type of dissolution and annulment, and the validity of an annulment is not dependent on the knowledge of the other party'. If the husband divorces her then has sex with her, he is considered a fornicator. Any child they may then have is the wife's, not the husband's.

A ruling with implications for alimony

Sunnipath

http://qa.sunnipath.com/issue_view.asp?HD=3&ID=31 05&CATE=336

Answered by Shaykh Amjad Rasheed

Question:

If a man divorces a childless woman, is he obliged to support her after this?

Answer:

No, whether she has children or not. But he must support the children if they do not have money.

Male doctors should not touch or see female patients

Sunnipath
http://qa.sunnipath.com/issue_view.asp?HD=3&ID=1
4371&CATE=473

Answered by Shaykh Amjad Rasheed

Question:
Is a male doctor allowed to see or touch the bodies of women he is treating?
Does this ruling alter when Western legislation forbids discrimination on the basis of sex?

Answer:
Male doctors may not see or touch female patients, except under limited circumstances (when the male doctor is more skilful, or when female doctors charge more).

Western Anti-Discrimination Laws
A male doctor should seek exemption from anti-discrimination laws. If this is not possible, he may treat female patients under strict restrictions: if he can diagnose or treat by listening, he should do so; if only to look at the patient, he must do so; if he does look or touch, it should only be at the appropriate areas; 'his looking and touching must be free of any desire whatsoever'; he should never be alone with a female patient. In a less strict interpretation, he may look at her face and hands.

A husband has conjugal rights over his wife

SunniPath

http://qa.sunnipath.com/issue_view.asp?HD=11&ID=4087&CATE=117

Question ID: 4087; Date Published: July 03, 2005

Answered by Shaykh Faraz Rabbani

Question:
Since a husband can force his wife to have sex, why does she not possess the same right?

Answer:
Both partners have the right to have their physical needs met. 'The only difference is that the husband may "demand" this, while the wife cannot.' This is considered to be rooted in the difference between male and female sexual desire. Since the husband is the head of the family, only he can make such demands.
A man must, of course, engage in foreplay: 'Do not begin intercourse until she has experienced desire like the desire you experience, lest you fulfill your desires before she does.'

Husbands have the right to demand sex; wives do not

SunniPath

http://qa.sunnipath.com/issue_view.asp?HD=1&ID=1830&CATE=117

Question ID: 1830; Date Published: July 03, 2005

Answered by Shaykh Faraz Rabbani

Question:

This is much the same as the previous question, but the answer is more detailed. The questioner considers it a form of abuse for a man to force his wife to have sex and asks why the wife does not have the same right.

Answer:

The respondent starts by emphasising that sexual relations are of primary importance in marriage.

'However, there is a legal difference between the husband and wife's right to sex: the husband can demand sex, and the wife is obliged to agree unless there is a *genuine* physical or Shariah preventative. Even if she disagrees, he has the legal right to insist that she comply. While it is obligatory for the husband to fulfill his wife's sexual needs, she cannot *demand* that he have sex with her if he does not want to.'

This superior right of the husband is understood to avoid greater problems such as 'sexual politics', which can lead to unlawful things like masturbation.

The respondent then quotes the following saying of the Prophet: 'If a man calls his wife to bed and she refuses, and then he sleeps angry, the angels shall curse her until he awakens.'

'This is not a call to sexual abuse; rather, it is a call to happy marriages where each spouse rushes to fulfill the rights and desires of the other.'

A woman may not remain married to her husband if he leaves Islam

SunniPath

http://qa.sunnipath.com/issue_view.asp?HD=11&ID=1 5035&CATE=121

Question ID: 15035; Date Published: August 01, 2007

Answered by Ustadha Zaynab Ansari, SunniPath Academy Teacher

Question:

The questioner is a convert from Hinduism to Islam. Her parents arranged a marriage to her Hindu cousin, who also converted. However, after a year, he reverted to Hinduism. He remains a 'dear and loving husband'. Is she committing a sin if she stays with him, even though 'Our marriage would otherwise be a happy one'? [*It is clear that there are no grounds for divorce in UK law.*]

Answer:

The respondent sees no solution: if the husband rejects Islam, she must leave him: 'You need to talk to your husband and ascertain for a fact that he has, indeed, reverted back to Hinduism. If he denies this, then you have no reason to seek a divorce. If, however, he openly rejects Islam, then you cannot stay married to him.'

A husband may prohibit his wife from leaving the house

SunniPath

http://qa.sunnipath.com/issue_view.asp?HD=1&ID=86
38&CATE=121

Question ID: 8638; Date Published: February 23, 2006

Answered by Ustadha Zaynab Ansari, SunniPath
Academy Teacher

Question:

May a woman travel within her own city alone, for
shopping or to spend time with female friends? She
cites a friend's husband that only necessity permits a
woman to go outside. 'Work, Education, having fun
with friends is [sic] not considered a need.'

Answer:

Provided she stays within the city limits, a woman may
venture outside provided she has her husband's
permission. Men may go out to earn a living, but
'Women, on other hand, should avoid going out
unnecessarily'. She adds: 'Yes, a husband may prohibit
his wife from leaving the house. But he should only do
so if it's in his wife's best interests, and not as a means
of control and domination.'

Sharia law deprives non-Muslims of their share in an inheritance

SunniPath

http://qa.sunnipath.com/issue_view.asp?HD=1&ID=5704&CATE=9

Question ID: 5704; Date Published: September 27, 2005

Answered by Ustadha Zaynab Ansari, SunniPath Academy Teacher

Question:
The questioner is a convert from the US. He is married to a Muslim woman, but without children. He wants to know if his wife is entitled to all of his inheritance.

Answer:
One third of what he leaves can go to anyone. But the remaining two thirds must go to his wife, since she is the only Muslim family member.

Inheritance from non-Muslims prohibited
http://qa.sunnipath.com/issue_view.asp?HD=1&ID=465&CATE=9

Question ID: 465; Date Published: September 17, 2005

Answered by Shaykh Faraz Rabbani

Question:
The questioner is also a convert to Islam. She wants to know whether, if her (non-Muslim) father dies, she may inherit.

Answer:

The answer is unequivocal: all four schools of Islamic law agree that a Muslim may not inherit from a non-believer. According to the Prophet: 'A believer does not inherit from an unbeliever, and an unbeliever does not inherit from a believer.'

2. Ask Imam

Accessed from Jamia Madina Mosque, Hyde

Divorce does not require a witness; re-marriage involves the wife marrying and having sex with another man

Ask Imam

http://www.askimam.org/fatwa/fatwa.php?askid=2b4d aa1a81f26ee0c5821eb083c60bfc

Fatwa # 16999 from South Africa

Mufti Ebrahim Desai

Question

The questioner and her husband had a fight, in the course of which he pronounced the formula of divorce. They were alone at the time. She wants to know if she is now divorced.

Answer

The respondent answers that witnesses are not needed for a divorce to be valid. He argues that, if a triple divorce has been pronounced, the wife may not re-marry her husband until she has gone through a process called *halala*. Halala involves her waiting four months until it is clear she is not pregnant. Then she must marry a second man and have sex with him. He should then divorce her, she must wait another four months, and finally she may re-marry her first husband.

Can a man marry a second wife?

Ask Imam
http://www.askimam.org/fatwa/fatwa.php?askid=d710
9ceb95219f85a8cefe128af2b302
Fatwa # 114 from Other Country/Island

Mufti Ebrahim Desai

Question
A man's wife is infertile. May he marry a second wife without first divorcing the existing partner?

Answer
'According to Shari'ah, a Muslim male may have four wives simultaneously with the condition of maintaining equality among all his wives. Therefore, in principle, you can remarry without divorcing your wife.'

An answer in justification of child marriage

(The following text (pp. 85-92) is from the Madrasa In'aamiyyah site, where Ask Imam is based, and is recommended as an answer to a question about the early age of consummation of Muhammad's wife A'isha)

Madrasa In'aamiyah
The original question and basic fatwa
http://www.al-inaam.com/social/myaaisha.htm

'Sadly we currently see the efforts of the Christian missionary activity focused primarily on derailing Islam now more than any other period in history. Thus, we witness numerous travesties and parodies coming from them in their attempts to twist, manipulate and totally abuse historical and etymological facts. These polemics range from a variety of the utterly hilarious to the outright abusive and cruel. One such dishonest Christian missionary polemic has been the allegation of the young marriage of Aishah (radiAllahu Anha) to the Prophet Muhammad(sallallahu Alayhi wasallam). The missionaries try to accuse the Prophet of being a child molester, albeit in politically correct terms, due to the fact that Aishah (radiAllahu Anha) was betrothed (zawaj) at the age of 6 years old and the marriage was consummated (nikâh) a few years after the marriage at 9 years old when she was in full puberty. The lapse of time between the zawaj and nikâh of Aishah (radiAllahu Anha) clearly shows that her parents were waiting for her to reach puberty before her marriage was consummated. If it were not for the fact that some gullible Christians have been parroting

85

the claims without understanding the reasons behind it, we would have not even bothered with a refutation. Such a claim is based only on conjecture and moral relativism, and not on fact. This article seeks to refute the allegation, insha'allah.

'Puberty And Young Marriage In Semitic Culture

'The hilarity of the whole saga of Christian missionaries accusing the Prophet (sallallahu Alayhi wasallam) of committing 'child molestation' is that this contradicts the basic fact that a girl becomes a woman when she begins her menstruation cycle. The significance of menstruation that anyone with the slightest familiarity with physiology will tell you is that it is a sign that the girl is being prepared to become a mother.

Women reach puberty at different ages ranging from 8-12 years old depending on genetics, race and environment. We read that

> There is little difference in the size of boys and girls until the age of ten, the growth spurt at puberty starts earlier in girls but lasts longer in boys.[1]

'We also read that

> The first signs of puberty occur around age 9 or 10 in girls but closer to 12 in boys[.][2]

'Women in warmer environments reach puberty at a much earlier age than those in cold environments.

> The average temperature of the country or province is considered the chief factor here, not only with regard to menstruation but as regards the whole of sexual development at puberty.[3]

'*Marriage at the early years of puberty was acceptable in 7th century Arabia as it was the social norm in all Semitic cultures from the Israelites to the Arabs and all nations in between. According to Hâ-Talmûd Hâ-Bavlî, which the Jews regard as their 'oral Torah', Sanhedrin 76b clearly states that it is preferable that a woman be married when she has her first menses, and in Ketuvot 6a there are rules regarding sexual intercourse with girls who have not yet menstruated. This is further collaborated when Jim West, ThD, a Baptist minister, observes the following tradition of the Israelites:*

> *The wife was to be taken from within the larger family circle (usually at the outset of puberty or around the age of 13) in order to maintain the purity of the family line.[4]*

'*Puberty has always been a symbol of adulthood throughout history.*

> *Puberty is defined as the age or period at which a person is first capable of sexual reproduction, in other eras of history, a rite or celebration of this landmark event was a part of the culture.[5]*

'*The renowned sexologists, R.E.L. Masters and Allan Edwards, in their study of Afro-Asian sexual expression states the following*

> *Today, in many parts of North Africa, Arabia, and India, girls are wedded and bedded between the ages of five and nine; and no self-respecting female remains unmarried beyond the age of puberty.[6]*

'*Were There Any Objections to the Marriage of the Prophet (sallallahu Alayhi wasallam) to Aishah (radiAllahu Anha)?*

'*The answer to this is no. There are absolutely no records from Muslim, secular, or any other historical sources which even implicitly display anything other than utter joy from all parties involved over this marriage. Nabia Abbott describes the marriage of Aishah (radiAllahu Anha) to the Prophet (sallallahu Alayhi wasallam) as follows.*

> In no version is there any comment made on the disparity of the ages between Mohammed and Aishah or on the tender age of the bride who, at the most, could not have been over ten years old and who was still much enamoured with her play.[7]

'Even the well-known critical Orientalist, W. Montgomery Watt, said the following about the Prophet's moral character:

> From the standpoint of Muhammad's time, then, the allegations of treachery and sensuality cannot be maintained. His contemporaries did not find him morally defective in any way. On the contrary, some of the acts criticized by the modern Westerner show that Muhammad's standards were higher than those of his time.[8]

'Aside from the fact that no one was displeased with him or his actions, he was a paramount example of moral character in his society and time. Therefore, to judge the Prophet's morality based on the standards of our society and culture today is not only absurd, but also unfair.

'Marriage At Puberty Today

'The Prophet's contemporaries (both enemies and friends) clearly accepted the Prophet's marriage to Aishah (radiAllahu Anha) without any problem. We see the evidence for this by the lack of criticism against the marriage until modern times. However, a change in culture has caused the change in our times today.

> Even today in the 21st century, the age of sexual consent is still quite low in many places. In Japan, people can legally have sex at

age 13, and in Spain they can legally have sex at the age of 12 years old[9].

A 40-year-old man having sex with a 14-year-old woman may be a 'paedophile' in the United States, but neither in China today, where the age of consent is 14, nor in the United States in the last century. Biology is a much better standard by which to determine these things, not the arbitrariness of human culture. In the U.S. during the last century, the age of consent was 10 years old. California was the first state to change the age of consent to 14, which it did in 1889. After California, other U.S. states joined in and raised the age of consent too[10].

'Islam And the Age of Puberty

'Islam clearly teaches that adulthood starts when a person have attained puberty.

'From the collection of Bukhari[11], we read the following tracts:

'The boy attaining the age of puberty and the validity of their witness and the Statement of Allâh:

> *And when the children among you attain the age of puberty, then let them also ask for permission (to enter).' Qur'ân 24:59.*

'Al Mughira said, 'I attained puberty at the age of twelve.' The attaining of puberty by women is with the start of menses, as is referred to by the Statement of Allâh:

> *'Such of your women as have passed the age of monthly courses, for them prescribed period if you have any doubts (about their periods) is three months...'[Qur'ân, 65:4]*

'Thus, it is part of Islam to acknowledge the coming of puberty as the start of adulthood. It is the time when the person has already matured and is ready the responsibilities

of an adult. So on what basis do the missionaries criticize the marriage of Aishah (radiAllahu Anha) since her marriage was consummated when she had reached puberty?

'We also read from the same source that

> *...Al-Hasan bin Salih said, 'I saw a neighbour of mine who became a grandmother at the age of twenty-one.'(1)*
>
> *(1) The note for this reference says: 'This women attained puberty at the age of nine and married to give birth to a daughter at ten; the daughter had the same experience.'[12]*

'Thus, it is clear that if the charge of "child molestation" were to be advanced against the Prophet (sallallahu Alayhi wasallam), we would also have to include all the Semitic people who accepted marriage at puberty as the norm.

'Conclusions

'We have thus seen that

'It was the norm of the Semitic society in 7th century Arabia to allow pubescent marriages.

'There was no reports of opposition to the Prophet's marriage to Aishah (radiAllahu Anha) either from his friends or his enemies.

'Even today, there are cultures who still allow pubescent marriage for their young women.

'In spite of facing these well-known facts, the missionaries would still have the audacity to point a finger at the Prophet Muhammad (sallallahu Alayhi wasallam) for immorality. Yet, it was he who had brought justice to the women of Arabia and raised them to a level they had not seen before in

their society, something which ancient civilizations have never done to their women.

'When Muhammad (sallallahu Alayhi wasallam) first became the Prophet of Islam, the pagans of Arabia had inherited a disregard for women as had been passed down among their Jewish and Christian neighbours. So disgraceful was it considered among them to be blessed with a female child that they would go so far as to bury this baby alive in order to avoid the disgrace associated with female children.

> *'When news is brought to one of them of (the birth of) a female (child) his face darkens and he is filled with inward grief! With shame does he hide himself from his people because of the bad news he has had! Shall he retain it on (sufferance and) contempt or bury it in the dust? Ah! what an evil (choice) they decide on!'[13]*

'Through the teachings of Islam, Muhammad (sallallahu Alayhi wasallam) put a swift and resounding end to this evil practice. God tells us that on the Day of Judgment, the female child will be questioned for what crime she was killed.

> *'When the female (infant) buried alive is questioned - for what crime she was killed.'[14]*

'Not only did Muhammad (sallallahu Alayhi wasallam) severely discouraged and condemned this act, he (sallallahu Alayhi wasallam) also used to teach them to respect and cherish their daughters and mothers as partners and sources of salvation for the men of their family.

'Abu Sa'id al-Khudri narrated that

'The Prophet (sallallahu Alayhi wasallam) said: 'If anyone cares for three daughters, disciplines them, marries them, and does good by them, he will enter Paradise.'[15]

91

'Abdullah the son of Abbas narrated that

'The Prophet (sallallahu Alayhi wasallam) said: 'If anyone has a female child, and does not bury her alive, or slight her, or prefer his male children over her, Allâh will bring him into Paradise.'[16]
'The Prophet (sallallahu Alayhi wasallam) is also cited in Saheeh Muslim as saying

> *'Whoever maintains two girls till they attain maturity, he and I will come on the Day of Resurrection like this'; and he joined his fingers.*

'In other words, if one loves the Messenger of God (sallallahu Alayhi wasallam) and wishes to be with him on the day of resurrection in heaven, then they should do good by their daughters. This is certainly not the act of a 'child molester', as the missionaries would like us to believe.

'Finally, we end this with a citation from the Holy Prophet (sallallahu Alayhi wasallam), who said

> *'I have come to defend the two oppressed peoples: women and orphans.'*

'The Prophet Muhammad (sallallahu Alayhi wasallam)

'Appendix: A married nine-year old in Thailand gives birth

'A news article from The New Straits Times, Malaysia dated 10th of March, 2001 about a nine-year old girl living in northern Thailand giving birth to a baby girl. The fact that a nine-year old girl is mature enough to give birth proves the point above about girls reaching puberty earlier than men.'

Mohd Elfie Nieshaem Juferi

A wife has no property rights in the event of divorce

Ask Imam
http://www.askimam.org/fatwa/fatwaList.php?pageN
um_rsFatwa=1&totalRows_rsFatwa=368&fid=8

Fatwa # 15855 from South Africa

Mufti Ebrahim Desai

Question
The questioner and his wife plan to divorce. Will she be entitled to a share in a property, even though he has paid all the fees? He lists his wife's shortcomings, from her refusal to satisfy his sexual needs to her foul temper.

Answer
Desai counsels against divorce, but argues that: 'If you have purchased the property with your money, the property belongs to you. Your wife does not have any share in the property even though the property is registered on [sic] her name as well. She should fear Allah and not unjustly claim a share of the property.'

A woman's concerns about halala are dismissed

Ask Imam
http://www.askimam.org/fatwa/fatwa.php?askid=1261
450b51bd84f7a2bbab0bc2db85fb

Fatwa # 15660 from Pakistan

Mufti Ebrahim Desai

Question

A woman writes to argue that the ruling of *halala* (through which she has to marry and have sex with another man before she can re-marry her first husband) represents a punishment for the wife.

Answer

The reply is prefaced by these words: 'The issue of halala can be viewed from many dimensions. Whichever dimension one tries to explain it with, in favour of it or against it, the reality remains that it is the order of Allah.' He goes on to argue that the wisdom of halala may be that it discourages men from issuing too hasty divorces, an argument that fails to address the fundamental issue that Islamic law makes it astonishingly easy for a man to divorce his wife.

Sharia law can override British courts

Ask Imam

http://www.askimam.org/fatwa/fatwa.php?askid=f073c fe9b4d93e57aca7def59f258f4c

Fatwa # 15522 from United Kingdom

Mufti Ebrahim Desai

Question

The questioner's wife has filed for divorce in a UK civil court and has applied for a Muslim divorce through the British Sharia Council. She has made various demands on him, which he refuses to fulfil unless she accepts all the rulings necessitated by an Islamic divorce (on child custody, for example). He wants her to repay the £40,000 that she has claimed through the civil court. He is a Pakistani national, she and their child have dual Pakistani/British citizenship.

Answer

It is argued that the husband has the right to stipulate the conditions applying to her Islamic divorce. (When a woman applies for divorce, it is known as a khula and is dependent on her husband's permission and the agreement of a sharia court.) He agrees that the husband should not pay her the £40,000, or that he may waive this claim if she drops her claim in the British court. Finally, the mufti states that: 'If you have incurred any other costs in defending the civil divorce applications, you can include that amount also in the Khula as her claim for divorce against you is un-Islamic.'

Rights of custody may differ from UK law

Ask Imam
http://www.askimam.org/fatwa/fatwa.php?askid=e6cc
e4f7dd507dbe862967ab610b93e0

Fatwa # 316 from Other Country/Island

Mufti Ebrahim Desai

Question

What are the Islamic laws on the custody and maintenance of children?

Answer

The respondent opens his response with a homily on love for children. He then enters directly into the conditions that allow a woman to have custody of her children, and those which cause her to forfeit it: 'The mother will receive the rights of custody with 5 conditions: She is (a) a free person; (b) adult; (c) sane; (d) trustworthy; (e) capable. Hence, the mother's right of custody is forfeited if: 1) she remarries a Ghayr Mahram [i.e. someone who could technically marry the child, which means almost any male person] of the child; 2) She demands remuneration for the upbringing of the child if there is another woman to rear the child without remuneration; 3) She does not attend to the child due to her leaving the house very often; 4) Openly indulges in sin and there is fear of the child being affected.' A disabled child must remain in the father's custody.

Note: The answer also lists all the degrees of relatives who may take custody in the absence of another in the chain. What he does not mention is that a mother may only have a male child till the age of seven and a female till she is nine.

A ruling that contravenes sex discrimination laws

Ask Imam

http://www.askimam.org/fatwa/fatwa.php?askid=0279 6533b386e959ddcd08164d61df84

Fatwa # 17034 from South Africa

Mufti Ebrahim Desai

Question
The questioner is a woman who has just opened a practice for touch therapy (only on affected areas) and wants to know if it is wrong to work on men.

Answer
In principle a doctor may treat someone of the opposite sex and confine work to the affected area, but in these times of immorality, she is discouraged from treating men in order to preserve herself from their 'evil intentions'.

A ruling that contravenes international legislation on freedom of movement

Ask Imam
http://www.askimam.org/fatwa/fatwa.php?askid=266 d996f4ea69e6c171fd0c46749e34e

Fatwa # 16992 from Singapore

Ml. Safraz Mohammed, Student Darul Iftaa
Checked and Approved by: Mufti Ebrahim Desai
Darul Iftaa, Madrassah In'aamiyyah

Question
The questioner's friend has told him that it is forbidden to migrate to a non-Muslim country. He has also been told that to work in a non-Muslim country is wrong, because it helps non-Muslims promote their economy.

Answer

The ruling differs according to the reason for migration. It is allowed if someone is fleeing from prosecution, imprisonment, etc.; if he has to seek work to earn a living; if he goes to the non-Muslim land for the purpose of spreading Islam. But if he can live comfortably in his own country, it is reprehensible for him to migrate for economic reasons. If someone seeks to adopt a non-Muslim nationality in order to imitate the non-believers, it is forbidden to do so.

Taking out insurance is forbidden. This conflicts with UK legislation which requires insurance for certain trades and professions. See the Employes' Liability (compulsory insurance) Act 1969 and the Road Traffic Act 1972.

Ask Imam

http://www.askimam.org/fatwa/fatwa.php?askid=f310 8c6b528f0d5af8d0277c72cb4284

Fatwa # 16980 from United Kingdom

Ml. Ishaq E. Moosa, Student Darul Iftaa; Checked and Approved by: Mufti Ebrahim Desai Darul Iftaa, Madrassah In'aamiyyah

Question

Is one allowed to take out building only insurance?

Answer

The respondent answers in the negative: 'All insurance policies are not permissible because they have three prohibited elements in it: interest, gambling and uncertainty.'

Medical insurance schemes are forbidden

Ask Imam

http://www.askimam.org/fatwa/fatwa.php?askid=4d17 e24678b9b90e652b2cbff1942c0a

Fatwa # 16743 from South Africa

Ml. Ishaq E. Moosa, Student Darul Iftaa; Checked and Approved by: Mufti Ebrahim Desai Darul Iftaa, Madrassah In'aamiyyah

Question
This question and answer session leads to the same conclusions as the one before it. The questioner asks about 'medical aids' (health insurance) which, they have heard, are prohibited (for Muslims) and enquires whether there are any that are sharia compliant.

Answer
The respondent attaches a transcript of a talk on this subject by Ebrahim Desai, dated 18 May 2008.
In it, Desai states, as above, that: 'All conventional medical Aid schemes are not permissible because they have three prohibited elements in it: interest, gambling and uncertainty.' He concludes by giving details of the Crescent Lifestyle Club, a non-interest scheme that is considered sharia compliant.

Insurance is forbidden, even if required by law

Ask Imam

http://www.askimam.org/fatwa/fatwa.php?askid=a11a4bbb842d8ecf2ae52423a7712968

Fatwa # 286 from Other Country/Island

Mufti Ebrahim Desai

Question
The questioner asks whether insurance is forbidden, and continues by asking: 'Even if it is required by law?'

Answer
As before, the questioner is told: 'All forms of Insurance is [sic] not permissible since these companies are based on Interest and gambling'. Desai does not qualify his answer in any way to take into account the second part of the question.

A discriminatory ruling on marriage to non-Muslims

Ask Imam

http://www.askimam.org/fatwa/fatwa.php?askid=91dfa203cd13f47509d2c47e2fb71974

Fatwa # 17317 from South Africa

Ml. Zakariyya bin Ahmed, Student Darul Iftaa; Checked and Approved by: Mufti Ebrahim Desai Darul Iftaa, Madrassah In'aamiyyah

Question

The questioner asks what Islam says about interfaith marriage, and gives the example of a Christian girl marrying a Muslim man.

Answer

The respondent says that one must seek for a religious partner who is compatible in other ways. Marrying a Jewish or Christian woman carries serious risks, particularly the possibility that the mother may bring her children up in her faith. It will be better if the Christian girl converts, but even that is not free of problems. Marrying a religious Muslim woman is recommended.

No requirement to register marriage according to the law of the country

Ask Imam

http://www.askimam.org/fatwa/fatwa.php?askid=9088 c4c0f557fc623f205f25dc276e23

Fatwa # 17264 from United Kingdom

Mufti Ebrahim Desai

Question

The questioner asks if a court [civil] marriage is necessary.

Answer

'It is not a requirement in Shariah to have the Islamic Marriage (Nikah) registered according to the law of the country.' It is not explained how legal registration of marriages can take place.

Ruling that implies polygamy is acceptable, even if against the law

Ask Imam
http://www.askimam.org/fatwa/fatwa.php?askid=1d45
67a59b2170c43071150403a41db5
Fatwa # 16744 from United States

Ml. Ehzaz Ajmeri, Student Darul Iftaa; Checked and Approved by: Mufti Ebrahim Desai Darul Iftaa, Madrassah In'aamiyyah

Question
The enquirer simply states that some imams in America will not sanction polygamous marriages, because they are against US law. He also states that these imams insist on Muslims having a civil marriage before the Muslim one, and asks what is the correct Islamic procedure.

Answer
The Mufti acknowledges that Muslims must obey civil law. But he continues by saying: 'It should be understood that the Islamic matrimonial system is not exactly identical to a normal civil marriage. According to *Shari'a* polygamy is permissible and a marriage can be concluded simply by the offer and acceptance taking place in front of two males or one male and two female witnesses.'

Discriminatory ruling on marrying a Shi'a

Ask Imam

http://www.askimam.org/fatwa/fatwa.php?askid=0ab5
66f2aadcf82982bab8c1e0918a91

Fatwa # 632 from Other Country/Island

Mufti Ebrahim Desai

Question
Can a Sunni Muslim woman marry a Shi'a man?

Answer
A flat no. 'Shi'as are not Muslims. Marriage with Shi'as
is invalid.'

Discriminatory ruling on renting from a church

Ask Imam

http://www.askimam.org/fatwa/fatwa.php?askid=8dc3
92aa5aed5771b58e9d8a967d202b

Fatwa # 17233 from United States

Mufti Ebrahim Desai

Question
The enquirer is a student who has taken accommodation near the campus and the mosque. However,
the apartment is owned by a church. Is it permissible to
stay, knowing that the rent probably goes towards
church maintenance and preaching activities.

Answer
'It is undesirable to hire the apartment belonging to the church.'

A Muslim lawyer should not always act in accordance with UK law where it contradicts sharia

Darul Iftaa, Leicester

http://www.daruliftaa.com/question.asp?txt_QuestionID=q-15573910

Muhammad ibn Adam Darul Iftaa Leicester, UK

Question
The questioner is about to start a career in law. Someone has told him that most aspects of English law would be forbidden to him to practise. Could he/she defend people of crimes (irrespective of guilt), and could they advocate rights for people such as homosexuals?

Answer
One should not help defend someone who is guilty of a crime. One must not help others gain a right prohibited by sharia or disapproved of by it. 'When practicing law, one must do so within the limits of Shariah. As such, one is not allowed to advocate rights that are incompatible with Islam, such as recovering interest money and fighting for the rights of homosexual and/or lesbians.'

Muslims may not work in insurance

Darul Iftaa, Leicester

http://daruliftaa.com/question.asp?txt_QuestionID=q-12174843

Question
The questioner has been working in insurance for two years. Is he allowed to continue in this work?

Answer
'It is always best to avoid working in the insurance industry.' Salary from an insurance company would be impermissible, since it originates in transactions of interest and gambling (which is how insurance is defined).

Car insurance may be allowed because legally required

Darul Iftaa, Leicester

http://www.daruliftaa.com/question.asp?txt_QuestionID=q-18594521

Muhammad ibn Adam Darul Iftaa Leicester, UK

Question
The questioner has listened to a sermon in which insurance was described as 'forbidden'. He seeks further information.

Answer
The Imam who gave the sermon was correct. The reason is that all forms of modern insurance involve interest and chance (gambling), which are prohibited.

At a conference of 150 scholars from 45 countries at the Islamic Fiqh Academy in Jeddah, all present agreed that this was so. However, since third-party car insurance is a legal requirement, it may be taken out.

Driving a taxi is all but prohibited, in breach of an individual's right to free legal employment

Darul Iftaa, Leicester
http://www.daruliftaa.com/question.asp?txt_QuestionID=q-18054715

Muhammad ibn Adam Darul Iftaa Leicester, UK

Question
The questioner has been unemployed for almost a year, but needs money for university. He doesn't want to take out a student loan, because it will carry interest. He has a car and wants to know if he can take up work as a cab driver. He does not have a taxi driver's licence.

Answer
The answer concentrates on the lack of a licence, rather than advising the questioner to get one. However, even if the work is unlawful, the income from it is not. Moral reasons for not working in cabs are given: 'Then there is the aspect of, being a cab-driver in itself being detested, for it may entail carrying passengers to the pubs and clubs, especially on weekends. They may in a bad state of intoxication, half naked, etc. One will have to be very vigilant in lowering the gaze from semi-naked women.'

106

Restrictions on being a police officer

Darul Iftaa, Leicester

http://www.daruliftaa.com/question.asp?txt_QuestionID=q-19054240

Muhammad ibn Adam Darul Iftaa Leicester, UK

Question
'Is it permitted to be a police officer in the West, given that you may have to implement laws that are against Islam?'

Answer
In principle, this is permissible, since it involves the performance of socially useful deeds. But if it involves anything that goes against the sharia, it is forbidden. If one can avoid anything that is against Islamic teachings, it is permissible.

Ambiguous ruling on paying tax

Darul Iftaa, Leicester

http://www.daruliftaa.com/question.asp?txt_QuestionID=q-19323489

Muhammad ibn Adam Darul Iftaa Leicester, UK

Question
Can a self-employed person who deals in cash declare a lower income to the tax authorities, and pay tax on the lower amount?

Answer

The mufti acknowledges that, if taxation meets several criteria of fairness and simplicity, it must be paid in full. However, if a government is deemed to be taxing unfairly, the individual citizen may withhold tax, provided they do not lie to do this. 'Therefore, in your case, if you think that the government fails to comply with the above mentioned conditions, then you may evade the tax provided you do not lie, whether verbally or in writing... In paying tax, you may not be asked with regards to your earnings, thus you may be able to get away with it without having to lie.'

Severe restrictions on women venturing outside their homes and driving cars. This seems to contravene UK and European law on freedom of movement

Darul Iftaa, Leicester
http://www.daruliftaa.com/question.asp?txt_QuestionID=q-05355441

Muhammad ibn Adam Darul Iftaa Leicester, UK

Question
'Are women permitted to drive cars in the modern society?'

Answer
'A female is encouraged to remain within the confines of her home as much as possible. She should not come [out] of the home without need and necessity.' Driving cars is permissible under certain conditions: 'a) There is a genuine need. For example, the husband can not

drive due to some reason or there is an emergency, etc... This shows that at times when the husband is being chauffer-driven [sic] by his wife, it will not be permissible. b) There is no alternative. c) There is no apparent fear of life or respect. If there is just the possibility, then it would be permissible.... d) The rules of Hijab are fully observed. e) If she is driving without the company of any of her Mahrams [those who cannot marry her, such as her father], then it should only be within 48 miles.... However, to avoid it is always advisable; rather staying within the home (as much as possible) and not emerging outside should be practice.'

Restrictions on an adult woman to marry whomever she chooses

Darul Iftaa, Leicester

http://www.daruliftaa.com/question.asp?txt_QuestionID=q-17113335

Muhammad ibn Adam Darul Iftaa Leicester, UK

Question
Can a woman who has been divorced marry a new husband against the wishes of her parents?

Answer
A lengthy answer follows. In principle, a free, sane, adult woman may marry without a guardian so long as her proposed husband is a legal and suitable match. If he is not, the marriage will be invalid. This applies to the Hanafi school of law. The other three schools do not permit a woman to marry without her guardian's

consent, and even the Hanafis think it would be better for the woman not to marry. 'As for appropriateness, it is inappropriate and against the Sunna, in normal situations, for a woman to marry without her guardian's approval.'

It is wrong to reject polygamy

Darul Iftaa, Leicester
http://www.daruliftaa.com/question.asp?txt_QuestionID=q-11395536

Muhammad ibn Adam Darul Iftaa Leicester, UK

Question
The questioner has received a proposal of marriage from a respected shaykh. An intermediary has told her that the shaykh's first wife has given permission for him to take a second. 'Although, polygamy is permissible in Islam, is it advised, especially when the person concerned is a religious scholar? Please advise.'

Answer
The mufti indicates that Muslims go to two extremes over polygamy. Some take it lightly and take second and third wives without much thought. Others deny that it is permissible at all. 'Many modernist Muslims and some others cannot tolerate the fact that Islam allows a man to marry a second wife after fulfilling the strict condition of fair treatment. Some consider polygamy to be abrogated, outdated or not suited to our times... Even "practising" Muslims unfortunately become involved in such absurd judgments...

However, polygamy is completely permissible in Islam (provided its conditions are met) and not something that is absurd, illogical or blameworthy. It is a serious crime to look down upon someone who takes on a second wife or condemn him. Criticizing and condemning someone merely for practicing polygamy is in reality being critical of the law of Allah Most High... If you are happy being a second wife and you have thought over all of the above-mentioned aspects and scenarios, then you may accept the proposal and marry him. With or without his first wife's consent, your marriage with him will be valid.'

Islamic law of legitimacy has implications for inheritance and contradicts the Legitimacy Act 1976[1]

Darul Iftaa, Leicester
http://www.daruliftaa.com/question.asp?txt_QuestionID=q-12154380

Muhammad ibn Adam Darul Iftaa Leicester, UK

Question
Two Muslims had a child out of wedlock, but are now married. The husband is the child's biological father. Is

---

1 Clause 2: Subject to the following provisions of this Act, where the parents of an illegitimate person marry one another, the marriage shall, if the father of the illegitimate person is at the date of marriage domiciled in England and Wales, render that person, if living, legitimate from the date of the marriage.

the child considered illegitimate, and will it inherit from him?

Answer

If the child had been born before the marriage took place, it would be illegitimate. Paternity would not rest with the child's father, even though he married the mother. Such a child will not inherit. A bequest of up to one third of one's wealth may, however, be made.

A woman may not leave her home without her husband's consent. This seems to constitute an illegal form of coercion or false imprisonment in UK law

Darul Iftaa, Leicester
http://www.daruliftaa.com/question.asp?txt_QuestionID=q-17551428

Muhammad ibn Adam Darul Iftaa Leicester, UK

Question

A man writes to ask if it is right for his wife to move to separate accommodation with her children while he is working in the Gulf. She has moved on the advice of her parents, but without her husband's permission, motivated by differences with some of his relatives.

Answer

'As for the wife, it is not permissible for her to leave her husband's house without his consent.' A wife who disobeys her husband, especially in leaving the house without his permission, is 'disloyal', based on a famous Qur'anic verse. Such a woman may not receive financial support from her husband, 'for entitlement to financial support is due to remaining and restricting herself to the husband's home'. Nevertheless, a wife has the right to a separate home or separate living quarters within the marital home.

Legal adoption is prohibited. An adopted child may not inherit from adoptive parents

Darul Iftaa, Leicester
http://www.daruliftaa.com/question.asp?txt_QuestionI D=q-16385935

Muhammad ibn Adam Darul Iftaa Leicester, UK

Question
'What is the sharia law ruling on adopting a child?

Answer
It is commendable to adopt a child. But it must be borne in mind that the lineage of the adopted child does not become that of its parents. 'Adoption of a child has no legal effect in Shariah... Legal adoption is not permissible... With regards to inheritance, the child will not inherit from the family.'

Discriminatory ruling on Muslim-Hindu marriage

Darul Iftaa, Leicester
http://www.daruliftaa.com/question.asp?txt_QuestionI D=q-15374665

Muhammad ibn Adam Darul Iftaa Leicester, UK

Question

The questioner, writing from the Netherlands, has a son who wants to marry a Hindu girl. She has agreed to convert. However, the girl's parents want a Hindu wedding ceremony (but do not require the boy to convert). There is a fear that, if this cannot be done, the couple will marry according to civil law, and then what will become of them?

Answer

'It is not permissible for a Muslim to marry a Hindu girl unless she accepts Islam.' It would not be a valid marriage if contracted according to Hindu rituals. 'To attend the Hindu place of worship and contract the marriage according to the rituals and customs of their religion is something that can never be considered by a Muslim.' But a civil marriage is acceptable.

Discriminatory ruling on marriage with non-Muslims in general

Darul Iftaa, Leicester

http://www.daruliftaa.com/question.asp?txt_QuestionID=q-15261824

Muhammad ibn Adam Darul Iftaa Leicester, UK

Question

Why can young Muslim women not marry outside the faith?

Answer

'Inter-marriage between Muslims and non-Muslims is something that has been clearly prohibited in the Qur'an and Sunnah, thus not permissible in any way.' A principal reason for this (which is a Qur'anic ruling) is the fear that love for a non-Muslim partner may influence a Muslim to be soft on unbelief, which may lead him/her to hell. The only exception is that Muslim men may marry Jewish and Christian women, subject to certain conditions. Why may Muslim women not marry Jews or Christians? 'The answer to this question is that, women are somewhat weak and emotional by nature. Then, the husband has also been given a caretaking and controlling role over the wife. As such, it is very likely that the Muslim wife may fall prey and become impressed with her husband's faith.'

A man may coerce his wife to have sex

Darul Iftaa, Leicester
http://www.daruliftaa.com/question.asp?txt_QuestionID=q-07335282

Muhammad ibn Adam Darul Iftaa Leicester, UK

Question

'What are the rights of woman after marriage? If the husband calls the wife to bed, can she say no? Does the husband need the wife's consent to have Intercourse? If there is no consent, and the wife doesn't want to, and he forces himself over her, isn't that rape?'

Answer

The mufti starts by quoting a well-known Prophetic tradition: 'When a man calls his wife for sexual intimacy and she refuses him, thus he spends the night in anger, the angels curse her until morning.' He follows it with another: 'When a man calls his wife for sexual intimacy, she should come, even if she is (busy) in the cooking area.' And a third: 'By the one in whose hands is my life, there is not a man who calls his wife for sexual intimacy and she refuses him except that Allah becomes angry with her until her husband is pleased with her.' To sum up, it is unlawful for a wife to deny her husband his conjugal rights except for a valid reason. This does not mean the husband has the right to force himself on her. 'If the wife is ill, fears physical harm or she is emotionally drained, etc; she will not be obliged to comply with her husband's request for sexual intimacy.' It is not made clear what the wife's rights are should she have invalid reasons for refusing sex, whatever these may be.

Restrictions placed on a divorced woman's right to take a child in her custody abroad or to retain custody after seven or nine years

Darul Iftaa, Leicester
http://www.daruliftaa.com/question.asp?txt_QuestionID=q-18054719

Muhammad ibn Adam Darul Iftaa Leicester, UK

Question

After their divorce, the questioner's ex-wife took their child from England (where he lives) to Canada (her native country). He is unable to provide the child with support. He cannot move to Canada because he is not allowed to work there. Is she allowed to remain there without his permission?

Answer

The mother has the right of custody to the age of seven for a male child and nine for a girl. After that, the father's right overrides hers. A divorced woman may move with her child from a village to a nearby town, but not from the town to a village. She may also move from a city to another city, provided the latter is her home town and her marriage was contracted there. If either of these conditions is not met, she may not move.

A marriage carried out in a civil registry may be considered invalid if it does not conform to Islamic conditions, even where the wife is a Christian

IslamOnline

http://www.islamonline.com/news/newsfull.php?newi
d=115789

Shaykh Muhammed Salih Al-Munajjid

Question

The questioner is a Christian woman, recently married to a Muslim man. The couple had a civil marriage and did not have an Islamic marriage. She has been surprised to discover that this marriage is not considered 'real' in Muslim terms.

Answer:
The marriage is only valid if her guardian says 'I offer my daughter in marriage to you'; the husband says 'I accept'; and the contract was done before two Muslim witnesses. If these have not been met, they will have to marry again.

Sharia law takes priority over secular law

IslamOnline
http://www.islamonline.com/news/newsfull.php?newid=106502

Question
A Muslim woman has separated from her husband and is using Swiss law to sustain a situation in which she is not divorced but is entitled to over half her husband's salary. Is it correct for her to use civil law rather than sharia? The questioner believes that this woman's aim in acting like this is to prevent her husband from marrying again. However, it appears that the husband divorced her [understood: Islamically] over a year previously.

Answer
'It is not permissible to refer for judgment to anything but the shareeah of Allaah'. There follows a long and complex argument. Recourse to any but Islamic law is ruled out in absolute terms: 'The one who seeks judgement from anyone other than Allah and His

Messenger is not a believer, and is either an unbeliever who is beyond the pale of Islam or an unbeliever in the sense of lesser unbelief. Divorce takes place when the husband pronounces it, not when another authority (such as a secular judge) decrees it: 'It is not permissible to turn to man-made laws in order to prevent a man from doing that which Allah has permitted'. The wife is no longer entitled to maintenance, even if the civil court says she is.

Islamic punishments may be suspended in a non-Muslim society, but can never be cancelled and may be implemented when the right time comes

IslamOnline.net Ask the Scholar

http://www.islamonline.net/servlet/Satellite?cid=11195 03549294&pagename=IslamOnline-English-Ask_Scholar%2FFatwaE%2FFatwaEAskTheScholar

Question
How can Muslims enforce sharia penalties for crimes such as adultery, while living in non-Muslim countries?

Answer
'Muslims should adopt a kind and wise approach. This, however, does not imply abandoning criminal penalties or canceling them. These penalties represent a part of Islam that cannot be revoked... The enforcement or implementation of *hudud* law would have to be postponed and upheld, not to be abandoned as suggested in your question.'

A ruling that might be taken to justify the extra-judicial killing of someone deemed a spy or traitor (e.g. a British Muslim serviceman)

IslamOnline.net Ask the Scholar
http://www.islamonline.net/servlet/Satellite?cid=11195
03548256&pagename=IslamOnline-English-
Ask_Scholar%2FFatwaE%2FFatwaEAskTheScholar

Question
How should Muslims deal with spies and traitors, such as Palestinians who inform on terrorist organizations?

Answer
'If a person is known for certain to be a spy who informs the enemies of Islam against the Muslim fighters, he is to be executed.'

Fighting Americans (and British) a legal obligation (a ruling that could be used to justify terror attacks in Western countries)

IslamOnline.net Ask the Scholar
http://www.islamonline.net/servlet/Satellite?cid=11195
03546834&pagename=IslamOnline-English-
Ask_Scholar%2FFatwaE%2FFatwaEAskTheScholar

Question
The questioner is a young Syrian who says his fellow youth are agitated by the issue of jihad against US-led forces. He asks an opinion about those who claim resistance is futile and will lead to mass suicide.

Answer

The Americans have not defeated Islam. Thus, 'Muslims have to resist the invading forces by all possible means.' The mufti cites Shaykh Faysal Mawlawi: 'fighting against the enemies who are invading Muslim countries is a legal obligation, and whoever gets killed in the course of such fighting is a martyr or *shahid* in the Cause of Allah. Muslims are enjoined to prepare whatever they can to resist invading forces, not to refrain from jihad until they prepare an army comparable to the enemy forces.'

Ruling sanctioning the payment of blood money in cases of manslaughter

IslamOnline.net Ask the Scholar
http://www.islamonline.net/servlet/Satellite?cid=11195
03544470&pagename=IslamOnline-English-
Ask_Scholar%2FFatwaE%2FFatwaEAskTheScholar

Question

A father has accidentally killed his two-year-old son. Does he have to pay blood money as well as *kaffara* (a gift made to seek forgiveness, expiate a sin)? Must he seek a waiver from one or more of the child's heirs?

Answer

The father must pay the blood money to the close relatives of the son. He may ask for a waiver from them.

A ruling on several extreme punishments for homosexuals, which could motivate beatings or worse

Islam Online
http://www.islamonline.net/servlet/Satellite?cid=11195
03545556&pagename=IslamOnline-English-
Ask_Scholar%2FFatwaE%2FFatwaEAskTheScholar

Question
The questioner has read how an Iranian man was convicted of raping and killing his 16-year-old nephew, and sentenced to be thrown off a cliff in a sack; if he were to survive that, he would be hanged.

Answer
Each crime (murder, homosexual rape) merits the death penalty. 'Homosexuality, moreover, is an abomination and a grave sin.' Different penalties exist for homosexuality: 'in the Hanafi school of thought, **the homosexual is punished through harsh beating,** and if he/she repeats the act, death penalty is to be applied. As for the Shafi`i school of thought, the homosexual receives the same punishment of adultery (if he/she is married) or fornication (if not married). This means, that if the homosexual is married, he/she is stoned to death, while if single, he/she is whipped 100 times.' Burning and stoning are also cited as possible punishments

Discriminatory ruling on marriage of a Muslim man to a Hindu woman

Ask an Alim, Leicester
http://www.islamiccentre.org/index.php?option=com_c
ontent&task=view&id=496&Itemid=25

Question:
Can a Muslim boy marry a Hindu girl without her conversion? She may convert later.

Answer:
'A male Muslim cannot marry a polytheist. Both partners must be Muslims at the time of marriage.'

Discriminatory ruling on marriage to a heretical Muslim

Ask an Alim, Leicester
http://www.islamiccentre.org/index.php?option=com_c
ontent&task=view&id=459&Itemid=25

Question
Is it permitted to marry a Shi'i, Wahhabi, or Deobandi?

Answer:
'It is wrong for a woman to marry a Shia, who have distorted and incorrect beliefs about the Prophet, and his beloved companions. The same applies to any religious sect that hold heretic and incorrect doctrines about Allah, His Messenger and His Sharia.'

Ruling denying a woman the right to fertility treatment

Ask an Alim, Leicester
http://www.islamiccentre.org/index.php?option=com_c
ontent&task=view&id=397&Itemid=25

Question
'Is it permissible for a Muslim woman to have fertility treatment using a donor egg from another Muslim or non-Muslim woman?'

Answer
Scholars dislike this practice. Other means should be sought.

A woman cannot marry without a male guardian present

Islamic Shariah Council
http://www.islamic-sharia.org/marriage-fiqh-of-
marriage-life/is-the-marriage-valid-if-the-wali-is-not-
pre-2.html

Question
Is a marriage valid if the woman does not have her guardian present?

Answer
'According to the opinion held by most of the scholars, the consent of the woman's guardian is needed at the time of the marriage along with the two witnesses. Therefore, it would be held as invalid.'

The mere intention to divorce is sufficient, regardless of wording

Islamic Shariah Council

http://www.islamic-sharia.org/marriage-fiqh-of-marriage-life/if-my-marriage-has-been-broken-due-to-me-saying-i-will-not-bring-you.html

Question

The questioner wants to know if his marriage has ended because he declared while angry 'If you go today, I will not bring you [back]' and later saying to his friends 'she's gone, finished'.

Answer

It entirely depends on the questioner's intention. If he did not intend divorce, he is not divorced, but if he did, then he is.

Polygamous marriage to be maintained even in UK

Islamic Shariah Council

http://www.islamic-sharia.org/marriage-fatwas-related-to-women/validity-of-polygynous-marriage.html

Question

If someone has married more than one wife legally in a Muslim country, will his marriages be valid in the UK?

Answer

'He should try to keep both wives. Either visiting the one, in her Muslim homeland from time to time if he can afford to do so or to bring one of them to U.K.

through a valid visa. Just emigration to U.K., is not a valid reason to divorce one of them.'

A husband excused alimony payments when an irrevocable divorce is pronounced

Islamic Shariah Council
http://www.islamic-sharia.org/divorce-talaq/talaq-bain-3.html

Question
A woman says she has received a full divorce from Dewsbury Sharia Council. She is told it is a 'talaq bain' and wants to know what this means. Is she entitled to financial support from her husband during the four months following the divorce?

Answer
Talaq bain means that the four months have expired and your marital relationship has completely ended. Therefore financial help will not be due from your husband.

A long fatwa arguing that sharia law is immutable

Islamic Shariah Council
http://www.islamic-sharia.org/general/deeming-shariah-islamic-law-as-incompetent-2.html

Introduction

'The reason behind our existence is submission to (God) and to His Laws whether we understand the wisdom behind each and every single one of them or not. Our role is not to question Allah... His Laws are perfect and are there for us as a test.'

Question one
'What is the Islamic ruling on statements stating the shariah law as barbaric and what is the ruling on saying Hudood [criminal penalties] are incompatible with contemporary life?'

Answer
'Belittling them or calling them as out-of-date constitutes disbelief... If you were to ask: "is every single shariah law unchangeable"? We say that shariah law is constituted in two segments:
1) Laws which are fixed for certain crimes such as adultery, murder, theft etc
2) Laws which are not fixed and are executed based up [sic] liaising between individual and society such as drinking wine etc. These laws or punishments are initiated by religious scholars or supreme leader who can choose to implement various methods for such actions such as either to lash them, or expel them from country or imprison them etc.

'Modern Western civilization is truly barbaric (atomic weapons etc.) and Islamic punishments are greater deterrents to crime.'